BETTER DREAMS

BETTER DREAMS

BOOST YOUR **SUBCONSCIOUS** FOR **SUCCESS**

BY

KURT GASSNER

My-mindguide.com

Better Dreams
Kurt Gassner

Impressum
My-mindguide – The publishing trademarke of trendguide Capital
GmbH, Klenzestr. 42a, 80469 Munich, Germany.

Reg. Nr. HRB Munich 206639, VAT 152 123 159, CEO: Kurt
Friedrich Gassner
Web: www.my-mindguide.com, mail: gassner@my-mindguide.com

Paperback ISBN: 978-3-98793-923-5
Hardback ISBN: 978-3-949978-75-3

"Truth itself only can be reached within one through the most profound meditation and conscious"

-Buddha-

Dedication

To all of you having problems sleeping. Workaholics, nocturnals, and people that, at some point in their lives, have been through times when sleeping well became something unreachable and thought they were alone or hopeless.

Table of Contents

Introduction

The mystery of sleep has been the focus of several studies and investigations since human beings evolved into Homo sapiens. The sleep patterns of many living beings have been scientifically explored by observing behaviors regarding sleep functions. Although important discoveries about sleep have been made, the question of why we sleep has brought forth multiple theories to date.

This is what I will elucidate in this book based on my experience of more than 40 years as an advertising consultant dealing with clients of all kinds. During my career, I have had the opportunity to observe hundreds of personalities and have received countless confidences regarding personal conflicts.

These close interactions with people of different statuses—from workers to managers who held high positions—were crucial in observing something they all had in common: they did not enjoy a good sleep and minimized the fact they did not rest enough or did not rest well. For this reason, and in relation to what I observed, they lived under constant stress. These inquiries led me to begin my research about sleep. I aim to answer the following questions: 1) How important is sleep, and how is mind's performance affected by poor sleep habits? and 2) How does sleeping well relate to success?

I take this opportunity to thank you for reading these pages. In them, I have incorporated what I learned across 40 years of experience as a creative director, owner of advertising agencies in Munich, Vienna, Kitzbühel, USA, Los Angeles, Netch Creative, and consultant. These positions allowed me to interact with countless people, in which I had the opportunity to analyze and listen to their most common complaints: "I am very tired"; "I only slept four or five hours maximum"; "Stress and responsibilities keep me up at night!"

During my consulting days, I occasionally found myself in that same situation. So, I decided to investigate why managers, people in administrative positions, housewives, artists, athletes, or movie stars, all develop—in the long run—some sleeping disorders. I eventually learned about hypnotherapy and meditation— practices that added to yoga habits and preventing those who engage in such habits from being part of the statistics of people with sleep problems.

For years, I investigated how the mind can help us or harm us. It has the power to hack false beliefs and install positive ones in our subconscious. The importance of the present moment and mindfulness can help prove my theory: A healthy sleep pattern, meditation, hypnotherapy, and physical care (yoga in my case) are essential tools for living up to your potential and achieving your most precious goals.

This is the result: a compendium of knowledge under the microscope of science. This same science has recognized the human mind as the hub that houses all our emotions and processes the ways in which they affect the decisions we make daily.

When you finish reading this book, you will have a powerful tool in your hands where you understand the importance of sleeping well and correctly. You will know what the phases of sleep are and what to do to achieve true rest.

You will understand what happens to your physical and mental body when you don't get enough rest. As a result, you'll be in a foul mood, irritable, and have no desire to achieve anything. You will learn how sleep interruptions keep you from being happy, leading to symptoms that can provoke heart complications, diabetes, erratic metabolism, and chronic depression.

I can assure you that all the problems you may be experiencing as a result of lack of rest can be corrected. I will demonstrate how hypnotherapy, meditation, and healthy habits helped me and led me to success, and to becoming the creator of my own brand and the author of several self-help books. But what I am most proud of is that I have been able to help thousands of people stabilize their lives through proper rest and self-serving thoughts.

Stay with me and allow me to show you the paths I have walked to reach goals that seemed impossible—but goals that have finally led me to a satisfying position in life. I can and want to share these unlimited resources with you so you discover the many possibilities you have within yourself and start using them to better yourself and your life.

People are capable, at any time in their lives, of doing what they Dream of.
My-mindguide.com

Chapter 1

The Power of Good and Productive Sleep.

Subconscious

The power of our mind goes beyond simply producing thoughts. Our mind is much greater and more powerful than we can imagine.

In the depths of our mind, below consciousness, there is a universe invisible to the naked eye where we bury our fears, insecurities, and our most cherished dreams and illusions. This is our subconscious or unconscious mind. Although the subconscious mind has been surrounded by a mysterious cloak for a long time, there are techniques now that allow us to reach this plane of the mind to enhance our psychological balance and achieve our goals.

The mind (conscious and unconscious) is variable and unique to each human being, depending on the moods and feelings of the individual. It responds to the information it's been exposed to, and when processing it, absorbs it and fills the individual with knowledge, which is often negative or pragmatic.

HOW MANY MINDS EXIST WITHIN US?

The Conscious Mind: Within the conscious mind evolves intelligence. Thus, we obtain knowledge, and it allows us to make decisions based on logical analyses. Many times, the conscious mind makes use of stored memories. Since it develops as time goes by, we always have more memories to store and hold onto.

The Subconscious Mind: It is the emotional mind. It is led by pleasure, feelings (love, hate), and the heart. Things we do and think every day create a neural relationship with the subconscious mind.

When, for instance, we change the layout of the furniture in our living room or anywhere in the house, it takes us more than a day to familiarize ourselves with the new arrangement. This happens because the neural connection was strengthened, and we subconsciously knew where each piece of furniture was placed before. The same applies to feelings: when we get used to spending time with another person, our subconscious strengthens the neural connections to that person. This behavior also applies to pets and objects.

The subconscious mind has access to your memories in ways the conscious mind does not. Memories that you assumed were forgotten can be brought back to the conscious mind if you gain access to it. These memories are stored and can be evoked by a sound, an image, or even a scent.

The Unconscious Mind: It is the most primitive—the one that keeps all the experiences that our species had gone through.

Since the beginning of mankind, the unconscious mind has been responsible for regulating our physiological functions, such as breathing, our heartbeat, and our blood circulation.

Now that you understand the inner workings of your mind and the way in which it was formed, it's time to teach you that you can make the most of it. In this chapter, we talk about the subconscious mind specifically because there are aspects that are projected to your conscious mind through it, meaning it revolves around how you feel, how you act, what you fear, or what pleases you.

You can use your subconscious mind as a tool to solve problems and even stimulate your creativity.

Your subconscious mind works all day long; it never stops—even when you are awake or asleep. But when you sleep, it takes over completely. Freed from the interference of daily life and external stimuli, your subconscious mind has almost all the resources of your brain at its disposal when you're asleep.

That being said, you must sleep properly. If you have not been able to control your insomnia or any sleep disorder, I suggest you do so first. Throughout this book, you will find several tips to help you get a beneficial rest. Remember, an erratic mind cannot be controlled so easily.

KNOW WHAT HAPPENS WHILE YOU SLEEP

The brain experiences important activity related to sleep function. However, this activity does not cease simply because the human body sleeps. On the contrary, when we sleep, a series of mechanisms are put into motion to give way to a very important task: sleep.

Specifically, when we sleep, a series of brain activities are triggered. This is measurable because this activity is nothing more than electrical impulses that can be visualized by an encephalogram.

While we're awake, two types of waves can be seen:
- Beta waves or beta activity. They are irregular and rapid waves that appear when the person is paying attention to his or her surroundings.
- Alpha waves or alpha activity, which is a pattern resulting from a person at rest.

When sleep occurs, the brain begins to emit specific waves, which are not visible during wakefulness. These waves are divided into phases:

- Phase 1: Alpha waves harmonize with a new activity, called theta. These are deep, low-frequency waves that indicate a state of extreme relaxation and drowsiness.

- Phase 2: The person is already asleep, and the brain's work in this phase gives rise to the sigma rhythm (also called sleep spindles) and K-complexes (a broad, negative wave followed by a small and positive wave). It's a phase of light sleep, from which it is easy to wake up.

- Phases three and four: These are the deep sleep phases called slow-wave sleep (delta waves). These phases allow the brain to rest and recover from the fatigue of the day. This period has a restorative function and lasts about 30 minutes.

- The REM phase appears about 90 minutes after the person is in a deep sleep. Throughout the night (if you sleep a minimum of eight hours), you can experience four to five REM periods.

Understanding the different stages of sleep is crucial if you want to learn how to take advantage of each phase. According to thousands of scientists and several pieces of research that have been carried out since the 1960s, the stage where the subconscious is more exposed to being observed and even modified is phase 1, where alpha waves are measurable: Their frequency ranges between eight and fourteen Hz. A person who has finished strenuous work and takes time to rest can enter an alpha state.

This is the state for meditation and is ideal for hypnotherapy. It is a state where you can access thoughts and memories that, being in a conscious state, your mind would normally block. It is there where you can install and uninstall the erroneous software (limiting beliefs) that prevent you from realizing your goals. Let's look at simple techniques to unblock the subconscious mind so you can access its benefits.

REPROGRAMMING THE SUBCONSCIOUS MIND

Reprogramming your mind through your subconscious means eliminating negative habits ingrained in you. This change of mentality or installation of new mental software will alter the direction of your life, allowing you to evolve by choosing the right path, or the path that serves you and your goals best. Replacing habits that have been ingrained in your mind for years is not easy. You may experience resistance in your subconscious, especially in the early stages. You must continue and persevere. This is the only way to make significant progress.

You can reprogram your subconscious mind while you sleep. Some of the most reliable techniques in doing so are as follows:

Concentrate on your breathing
This practice will help you relax and is the basis of all meditation. It is used to maintain the mind and physical body, while also inching you closer to the alpha state. This should become a habit, especially if you have trouble sleeping. Concentrating on your breathing will be the first step to accessing your subconscious mind.

Autosuggestion
Once you are relaxed and lying in bed, guide your mind towards your new habit or goal. A suggestion is a message from your conscious self to your subconscious mind to stimulate it to accept the positive aspects of your new standards and gradually make them part of your personality. This is a personal matter, since objectives and goals are unique to each individual. You should invest as much time as it takes to state your intentions, desires, and gratitude to ensure a positive outcome. Repeat the message(s) to yourself as deep sleep arrives. Only with repeated suggestions will the approach yield the desired results.

State and affirm in a positive way
Reading a statement you have written just before falling asleep helps implant an idea in your mind because the subconscious mind will continue to work on this statement while you sleep.

However, it must be done the right way: Target the area of your life that needs the most stability. Include your name in the affirmations; make them personal. Avoid negative words. Don't use words of comparison with other people (better, worse, more, less), and finally, ensure your affirmations are rooted in realistic, achievable goals.

Stating the affirmations repeatedly just before bedtime allows your subconscious to work on them while you sleep. This will help raise your vibrational frequency during sleep so that when you wake up in the morning, you will be bursting with positive energy. Recording them in your voice and listening to them while you sleep is a great strategy to implement, as the subconscious mind will be listening to its own voice.

Brain Reset
When you get home after a long day at work and your mind is filled with personal and work-related worries, you'll likely find it hard to rest, let alone fall into a deep sleep. Many people get home from work and start carrying out various tasks, whether it's fixing something in the garage or watering the plants, so that they can drain the adrenaline from the day.

Although this technique may be effective in the short-term, what if the negative thoughts simple ensue once your head hits the pillow? One proven technique to unwind after a difficult or busy day is called the brain reset download. This is where you simply take your notepad and start writing down everything that's bothering you. Include everything that comes to your mind, and pour all your immediate worries onto the page. By doing this, you are prompting the subconscious mind to eliminate all these thoughts from your memory while you sleep. This simple technique can help you permanently get rid of unwanted thoughts in your mind. Do this exercise several times a week.

Thankfulness also counts
Pushing away negativity and welcoming positivity can be accomplished by giving thanks. Gratitude is an instant energy booster. Your subconscious will continue to work on the same level of positivity when you are sleeping. This will ultimately influence how you approach and deal with the events of the day.

The UCLA Center for Developmental Mind Research has shown that gratitude changes our brain structure. It helps gray matter function more efficiently. By repeating this habit every night, you can ensure that negative practices are not stored in your subconscious mind.

With the mind filled with the positive energy that comes from gratitude, it becomes easier to eliminate harmful habits and beliefs, thus facilitating the reprogramming of the brain even after we fall asleep. As we give thanks and demonstrate gratitude daily, we will feel the changes and become happier people.

Chapter 2

How We Can Rewire Our Brain to Our Advantage.

Our brain is, without a doubt, the most complex organ in our body. It is involved in every function of our organism and is the primary organ responsible for keeping us alive.

We've seen how not sleeping well affects our physical and mental health, but there's one point specifically that is of utmost importance in this regard: If you want to be successful and accomplish your goals, your cognitive abilities, which reside in the brain, have to be at their best.

As previously explained, our subconscious mind is where messages and thoughts are stored according to lived experiences. These are peeked into the conscious mind—but only partly, and only if this information is relevant. The whole process, however, goes unnoticed. We do not understand how certain memories come to our minds, but we know that they influence how and why we act in certain ways.

It is an irrefutable fact that 90% of the information we possess—consciously and unconsciously—is stored in our minds. Science has always tried to find an explanation for events that, at first glance, seem miraculous and involve the recovery of the brain.

Through multiple studies, a consensus has finally been reached—at least in the field of psychological research. We have understood the concept of neuroplasticity[1], which refers to the ability of our brains to adapt according to the interaction and feedback they receive from the outside.

Some of these studies date back to the mid-20th century and focused on finding a logical explanation for the recovery of neurons, especially after a person experienced severe brain damage. That being said, we should not confuse neuroplasticity with neurogenesis, since neuroplasticity forms new connections and pathways in the brain, while neurogenesis is the ability to grow entirely new neurons. This topic is quite fascinating, and we could certainly devote an entire book to discussing it.

But the bottom line is it has been shown the brain can rewire itself, generating new pathways. In fact, it does so all the time.

What about the beliefs and mindsets we accept as deeply ingrained in our psyche? Is it possible to change and re-configure our thinking? There are theories supported by the facts described above that assure depressive or self-destructive behavior patterns can be interrupted and eradicated by stimulating neuroplasticity.

The brain would be doing what it always does, but the difference is that we would be directing the process to reinforce positive habits and behaviors while eliminating negative ones.

---

[1] https://hrcak.srce.hr/file/186735

A habit is installed in our brain so deep that we execute it almost automatically. Its consecutive practice leads it to become deeply rooted in our minds. It is not difficult to deduce that developing the habits we want is paramount, so they remain recorded at a subconscious level.

Accessing the subconscious mind is not easy, but it is not impossible, either. We live in a world where there is a lot of noise. Most people spend their days and nights with their cell phones in their hands, and this habit takes them away from their true selves and prevents them from connecting internally. There is this erroneous concept that things must have a tinge of immediacy. All information must be quick and accurate to move on to the next activity: looking at the mobile and immersing themselves in social networks.

Don't get me wrong—technology is an amazing tool, as long as you know how to manage it without falling into addictions that take us away from our reality, the present moment, and focusing on how to solve our problems. There are several ways to access the infinite torrent of information stored in the subconscious mind:

Hypnosis. This technique aims to access the subconscious mind through a series of instructions. The goal is to reach that information and modify habits and behaviors that need to be changed.

I am an expert in this technique in particular, and have used it with hundreds of people from all walks of life: businessmen, artists, athletes, assistants, or simply friends who are having a hard time. It is quite effective, and I will explain how it works:

When we enter a deep state of relaxation, our conscious mind cannot exert its stubborn dominance over us. At that moment, a part of our subconscious springs forth. This does not mean your subconscious is in control. The conscious mind is still there, but it withdraws, allowing the therapist to access areas that would normally remain hidden.

Hypnotherapy is so effective because it manages to circumvent the so-called critical factor, the barrier between the conscious and the subconscious. It accepts or rejects the new programs (beliefs) that we try to install. By doing its work of sensory focus, hypnosis allows the person to bring his or her attention to certain experiences in a state of relaxation, so it is easier to replace some perceptions or limiting thoughts with positive ones.

Meditation. Contrary to what many people believe, meditation does not require hours and hours of training. You don't have to dress like a Buddhist monk or go on long retreats to meditate. Meditation is nothing more than the practice of emerging yourself in a state of concentration in which you direct your focus on something specific, an object, a thought, your breathing, or your own consciousness.

In addition to relaxing and reducing stress, meditation regulates attention, a cognitive capacity that influences other mental processes, such as learning. Taking advantage of the plasticity of the human brain, meditation habits renew the connectivity between neurons and also modify certain neural structures.

In short, you can unlearn what you have learned and recharge your brain with new knowledge and positive attitudes that will undoubtedly lead you to success.

Positive visualization. The mind is our best ally and is at our disposal to achieve success in any goal we set for ourselves. However, it can also be our worst enemy if it is incorrectly programmed.

Visualizing is something we do constantly, maybe by remembering an event vividly that caused us pain. When you remember moments, conversations, or actions that happened, you get to experience some of that pain. Positive visualization is about seeing events that we would like to happen according to our plans, and with a positive outcome.

These three techniques are great for reprogramming your brain with positive thoughts, and I will dedicate a chapter to each one, thoroughly explaining how to get the best out of them.

The mind can reach a level of relaxation that will bring positive results in the short term, only by engaging in positive visualization exercises regularly before bedtime.

In Chapter 1, I explained at length what the subconscious is and how it affects our decision-making, the way we face difficulties, and how we live our lives. I am going to outline some activities that have been tried and tested by me as a counseling therapist and have worked successfully.

STRATEGIES TO GET THE MOST OUT OF OUR MINDS.

Practice positivity
Attitude impacts every field of life. Experts agree that attitude is the primary quality we must cultivate if we want to succeed in

life. Optimistic people develop a positive mental attitude, and this attitude makes individuals relate better on a personal level. Optimists get better jobs and have better salaries. Therefore, it is extremely beneficial to have an optimistic attitude if we want a fulfilling life, both personally and professionally.

However, we must also be realistic. Having a positive mental attitude should not be confused with being a smiling and happy person 24 hours a day, seven days a week. Of course, we will experience unforeseen events that cause us to think negatively. Maybe you find there is a downpour that afternoon when you scheduled your walk. Or maybe you find yourself in the middle of a traffic jam on the freeway that will probably make you late for an appointment. In short, inconveniences can and will arise in your daily routine.

What is the difference between a negative and positive person? Attitude is everything when it comes to facing any inconvenience. The person with a negative, pessimistic attitude will become hysterical. Not only that, but his or her frustration may spread to others, since anger in this regard have been proven to usually last approximately an hour and a half. If you also combine this with other events occurring during the day, it is not difficult to imagine what life is like for these people and how difficult it must be for them to achieve goals and succeed in their work and personal life.

People with a positive, optimistic attitude see the setbacks that come their way as out of their control. They focus on the things that are in their control only. As you assess a situation, you decide to feel good. For instance, you decide to do something productive while it's raining and postpone your walk for another time. Maybe you choose to listen to that audio for learning a new language while driving amid the freeway's jam.

Moving forward with a positive mental attitude is the key to not getting ourselves stuck in a loop of strategies that do not work, slowing down our productivity and all aspects of our existence.

At the end of a long day, ask yourself, are your thoughts a whining symphony or a list for better strategies to benefit your life in the long run?

Stop the pessimistic inner dialogue
To understand how our inner dialogue affects our life, we turn to an analogy to better illustrate this relationship: If you want to grow and obtain sunflowers, plant sunflower seeds, but if you want strawberries, plant strawberry seeds. The result will be flowers or fruits, depending on the seeds you plant.

Your internal dialogue is the seeds you plant. If your inner dialogue is filled with complaints and pessimism, then it is not surprising to encounter economic, health, and even relational challenges that keep you up at night. Language, in this case, is like a punishment we inflict on ourselves—statements of the future that we will undoubtedly see crystallized.

Phrases like, "I can't afford it"; "I don't get ahead"; "I feel worse every day"; "I'll never heal"; "It is too expensive for my budget"; and "I always end up alone" are some of the seeds you sow and cultivate each day. When it is time to harvest the fruits, you cannot expect abundance. If you have a mediocre mouth, you are going to have a mediocre life.

If you want to change these mental beliefs and daily habits for good, learn to sow different seeds so that only positive affirmations come out of your mouth and, therefore, profitable actions.

You do not have to be afraid to fail; making mistakes is human. What is failure? I agree with the concept that all results of any activity or interaction are achievements, whether they are part of the desired outcome or not.

I've experienced the unpleasant feeling associated with not achieving our goals. I know failure can produce anxiety, hindering our concentration and our cognitive abilities.

If we accept the premise that our thoughts create our reality—that we are the ones who generate our experiences in life—then we must inevitably accept responsibility for what happens to us, whether it's good or bad. Because, in the end, we, ourselves, have created these things.

The pressure to be superhuman in today's society is evident, but also unachievable. You need to be productive at work, organized, a good friend, fit, a good father, a good son, and so on. For women, the demand is even stronger, where the expectations are being a perfect mother, the ideal wife, and a tireless worker, while also being neat, fashionable, and presentable at all times. These are impossible standards for one human being to achieve.

When we do not succeed in any of these categories, we feel like failures. We feel that we do not meet the standards set for us—that we are obsolete. These high demands converge at rest time, making us rack our brains thinking about how to meet such standards. Certainly, this prevents us from resting properly at night. The next morning, we see the consequences of our internal battle when we look back at our reflections in the mirror.

We have to break away from this false and unnatural vision that society has imposed, forming an endless ladder that we can never reach the top of. The obsession with imitating movie artists, prominent athletes, and recently—the most harmful, in my opinion—influencers, will not help.

We live in a society where we demand too much of ourselves, as individuals and as a collective. This modus vivendi is a great source of stress. According to official figures, 80% of people living in big cities suffer from stress, and this percentage drops very little in less populated cities. Stress and anxiety translate into sleep disorders. It is proven that a high percentage of top executives in prominent companies suffer from insomnia or sleep problems. They have a firm belief that the stress in which they live is something normal they must experience if they want to achieve success.

Making mistakes is nothing more than learning by trial and error. Great athletes, the best artists, and movie directors know this. All of them have made many mistakes to reach the top.

One of the examples of falling and getting up was given by the great basketball star, Michael Jordan: "I can accept failure, everyone fails at something. But I can't accept not trying. To learn to succeed, you must first learn to fail."

Better Dreams

Chapter 3

The Power of a Restful Night.

Adequate sleep is related to the benefits of restorative sleep on both a physiological and psychological level. Sleeping incorrectly or too little can bring serious consequences for our body and brain, and, consequently, our mental health.

Resting is as necessary as eating healthy or exercising regularly. It is an indispensable biological function. In addition, we spend a third of our life sleeping, so it is better to do it well.

Sleep, like hunger, sexual behavior, intellectual performance, and mental health, is regulated by the biological clock we all possess, located in the hypothalamus. When this clock is activated, melatonin, the hormone that prepares the body for sleep, is secreted. If we sleep enough hours and wake up refreshed, there are many benefits for our health. However, if we drastically change our sleep habits, there is a high probability that we will experience fatigue, stress, moodiness, and often, anxiety.

CAN SLEEP BE AN ACCOUNTING LIABILITY?

"Last night I could not sleep! Don't worry, I will catch an hour of sleep in the afternoon."

This expression referring to the fact that perhaps we are indebted to sleep, and can later make up for that time, is typical of people who sleep poorly. When someone expresses this, what they really mean is: "It is true; I don't sleep well, but that does not prevent me from working normally." Sleep experts have described this attitude as sleep debt, and we all know that if we do not pay our debts back correctly, we start facing trouble. In this sense, this will lead us to lose control over our brain and body.

Now, is this loan to rest so harmless?
Specialists have compared an exhausted brain to a brain driving under the influence of alcohol, both of which operate in the same manner. In the United States alone, the number of people who have caused fatal accidents under the influence of liquor totals 95,000 people annually. (Approximately 68,000 men and 27,000 women who die each year from this cause.)

So, we can deduce that a person driving after a few hours of sleep will be just as dangerous as a person who is intoxicated. In road accidents, not everyone is under the influence of alcohol. However, it is very difficult to detect a driver who only fell asleep for four seconds and did not see the light change at the traffic light.

In the 1960s, more than 70% of people fell asleep before ten p.m. However, everything changed with the arrival of the 21st century. Between 40 and 45% of people stay awake past midnight, while 20% stay up until the wee hours of the morning. What changed? Technology. With the advent of the cell phone, the internet, and more recently, social media, it has become easier for people to log on and have all the information they need on a small screen that can keep them entertained for hours.

The problem is the average sleep time decreases every year. For example, it is now customary for professionals, such as doctors and nurses, to work 48 hours straight. How can a doctor who has not slept for two days have clear judgment? The individual's cognitive faculties diminish with a lack of sleep, as does his or her speed of response. Of course, a sufficient and restful sleep of no less than seven hours is extremely important to:

Reduce traffic accidents
Avoid the so-called four-second micro sleep. It has been proven that only four seconds are enough to cause a tragedy.

Be alert. If you are a health professional, you know what one or two nights of bad sleep can cause. For a physician, to have eight-hour shifts and sleep another eight hours in less than 24 hours is ideal. After all, physicians are human beings.

These are general issues, but it is different for each individual. Sleep affects men and women equally. So, if you don't work shifts and still have problems sleeping, either because of health disorders or because you stay glued to your cell phone or tablet, you should consider not being part of the negative statistics mentioned above.

BENEFITS OF SLEEPING WELL.

Renewed energy.
People who suffer from anxiety disorders or lack of concentration need to establish a healthy sleep routine of 7-8

hours. This routine will restore their energy and improve their mood, making them cheerful people with a better attitude and initiative to do their work, complete their studies, or engage in any pending undertaking.

Better mnemonic retention.
Deep sleep helps us retain information better, favoring capacity. A study published in *Psychological Science* affirms that sleeping well helps the mind absorb the information received long term. This is essential—especially for students or people with sensitive data manipulation jobs.

Conversely, if sleep is intermittent throughout the night, the ability to ingrain memories is reduced, and the person becomes forgetful and slow to remember things. The consequences of not sleeping well can be stress, anxiety, fatigue, drowsiness, tiredness during the day, poor ability to concentrate, slowness of response, slow reflexes, and so on.

When the wandering mind prevents us from sleeping.
We often go to sleep with the many events that occurred during the day playing in our minds: Issues with the children, the next mortgage or car insurance payment, our relationship with our partner, and so on. Whatever the concern may be, many people begin to look for solutions at this time. This is why you may experience tiredness, but when you are ready for bed, your mind is wide awake in a state of alertness, sorting through all the worries of the day.

Logically, your brain is activated. You have given it one or several problems to solve, and that is why the state of relaxation you were previously in vanished. The next day, your daily routine and pending activities take you away from those thoughts until you have some free time. Coincidentally, that free time comes the following night, and the cycle continues!

Many of you can identify with this situation. I have also experienced it on more than one occasion. So, these are some recommendations you can apply next time this happens to you:

First, identify the wandering thought. As soon as you notice your mind is wandering, looking for solutions, or planning what you are going to do, stop.

Second, take note of each issue and write it down. Next to it, jot down two or three actions to resolve it. If you have several concerns, do the same for all of them.

Third, go back to bed and disconnect your mind from those thoughts. Then, practice breathing exercises to gradually achieve a state of relaxation that will lead to peaceful rest.

Writing down both the problem and the possible solutions is a ritual that allows you to do your best. The day is over. To believe that your mind will produce a panacea for all your problems is illogical and unrealistic. Instead, you can rest, knowing you have already written down three possible solutions.

Remember to take your note sheet and carry it with you during the day. When is it time to revisit those thoughts? The moment you think of a solution you did not already write down. Pull out the sheet and write it.

If you have an immediate decision to make, pull out your notes, compare the pros and cons, and decide. That is the best way to free your mind and avoid that worry hanging over your head at the most inopportune time: bedtime.

Be pragmatic. Letting yourself go down blind alleys in your mind and repeating these scenarios is not a helpful mental exercise.

We know that there are situations in life that are more complicated, and they take more than a few notes to resolve. But there is a saying in Spanish that sums this up perfectly. It can be translated as: "Be productive before being engaging." It means take action instead of worrying endlessly.

If the solutions at hand (there is never a problem without a solution), do not satisfy us, it is useless to wander in search of an ideal scenario because all we will get is frustration. It is not a realistic approach and certainly will not solve the problem. Taking the best possible option under the circumstances.

Remember, if you cross one problem off your list, it is one problem less to deal with at bedtime.

USEFUL TIPS TO PREPARE OUR ENVIRONMENT TO REST

To have a restful night, we must first prepare the body for rest. There are several guidelines we can follow during the day—and even during the week—to prepare ourselves before putting our head on the pillow. Here, I mention the most recommended strategies to achieve a restful sleep:

- Establish a schedule in which you wake up and go to sleep at the same time every day and every night.
- Avoid naps after three p.m.
- Avoid caffeine and alcohol at night.
- Avoid nicotine.
- Exercise regularly. However, avoid doing it two to three hours before bedtime, especially high-impact or strenuous exercise. If you need to be active, choose a short walk about three hours before bedtime.
- Eat lightly. Some people don't eat dinner. However, it can interrupt your sleep at some point. You may feel hungry at an early hour—even at dawn—and it will make you wake up before your scheduled time.
- Make your bedroom comfortable, dark, quiet, and keep it at an optimal temperature—not too cold and not too hot.
- Check your bed. You may not be resting on an ergonomic mattress. Changing your current mattress to one of good quality—a semi-orthopedic mattress—can make a significant improvement in your sleep.
- Establish a habit that helps you relax before bedtime (e.g., reading or listening to music).
- Don't lie awake in bed tossing and turning for hours. If you can't fall asleep after 20 minutes, do something relaxing until you feel sleepy, such as meditating, reading, or listening to soft music.

As for how long you should sleep, it is good to always sleep at the same time. Sleeping at night is also much more beneficial. During the day, scientists and specialists advise taking a short nap to reactivate the organism and the brain. These naps, however, should not exceed half an hour.

DAILY ROUTINE MAKES BALANCED HABITS.

The human body is inclined to routine and responds to stability. Therefore, your body will benefit if you get up and go to bed at the same time every day, as many days as possible. Remember, sleep cannot be made up. Lost hours cannot be regained.

During childhood and adolescence, the human being sleeps more hours, although as we will see later, in the elderly, these hours decrease. Most people need six to eight hours, but this can change according to the individual's personal and work conditions, age, lifestyle, or health. So, it is necessary to observe your habits to know how much sleep you need to wake up energetic and rested.

THE HOURS IN WHICH YOU EAT ALSO COUNT.

The ultimate stimulant has always been believed to be coffee. However, tea, fizzy drinks, and high-sugar desserts are also stimulants, and consuming them can prevent us from falling asleep. Excessive consumption of these foods should be avoided, especially during an evening meal.

Chocolate is also a stimulant of the nervous system that can make you either sleepless or wake up earlier. In addition, it is advisable to reduce or avoid the consumption of alcohol or other alcoholic substances.

AVOID STIMULATING ACTIVITIES IN THE HOURS BEFORE GOING TO BED.

Sports and exercise are excessively stimulating just before bedtime; however, so is watching an action movie or getting maximum excitement from a television program. This influences our level of physiological activation. Many experts and doctors have argued that the habit of consuming audiovisual products increases the probability of suffering insomnia, mainly among people between ages 18 and 32.

To promote a restful night, we should choose relaxing activities before going to bed, such as listening to background music, taking a warm bath, light reading, or breathing exercises. What I recommend most is meditation. If you want to exercise, yoga is, by far, the best option, and I say this as a certified yoga and meditation teacher. Personally, these habits helped me enormously, and I have seen how they have helped dozens of people who have come to me for help, as well.

In future chapters, I address meditation and yoga as successful tools to recover sleep balance.

QUIET AND CALM COMMUNICATION IS BETTER THAN ARGUING AND FIGHTING.

The bed should not be considered a psychological consultation or a place to discuss differences with our partner. Essentially, if you have concerns preventing you from falling asleep, it is preferable to get up and set a time the next day to talk. In fact, it is always best to discuss our relationship in a neutral setting. The two of you can meet at lunch or after breakfast, but never discuss your problems right before bedtime.

AN OPTIMAL SLEEPING ROOM.

The conditions in which our bedroom is located when we go to sleep can predispose the quality of our sleep. In a perfect world, all members of the household would go to sleep at the same time. If that's not possible, it's enough to close the doors and windows of the room and be sure that the overall temperature in the room is ideal—not too hot and not too cold. As has been repeatedly mentioned, you should turn off your cell phone to avoid distraction, as well as all LED lights in the room. This measure is paramount, as these lights are detrimental to the REM phase or the segregation of melatonin in our body.

HOBBIES. THE BENEFITS OF HAVING THEM.

In the recent pandemic that has lasted more than two years, thousands of people presented symptoms of anxiety and depression. Therapists and psychologists around the world turned to counsel online patients. They sought to alleviate the effects of being locked up and, in many cases, away from family.

One of the most recurrent pieces of advice was to encourage individuals to pursue a hobby or interest. Inactivity can be demotivating and leads people to feel sad and lonely, which would be the manifestation of the first symptoms of depression.

To enjoy our life fully involves having time for ourselves. There's a special way to get in touch with what we like the most and, at the same time, take a break from everything that represents our boring routine. Hobbies or interests are small spaces of freedom. The time we dedicate to them is our real free time, the one in which we do what we enjoy. The purpose of these activities is not to obtain monetary remuneration, nor to fulfill an obligation, but to enjoy something we like. Dedicating our attention to something we love is a true stress-releasing stimulus.

Mental health specialists agree that having a hobby increases the quality of your life. It is a mechanism that balances and helps preserve physical and emotional health, avoiding in many cases that people manifest episodes of stress that can lead to a strong depression.

Coming home after doing something that we like and enjoy to the fullest will trigger a state of relaxation from the physical and emotional aspects of our minds. In turn, this will allow us to have a restful sleep.

Better Dreams

Chapter 4

Technological insomnia.

A BRIEF INTRODUCTION

Sleep is driven by a small, almond-sized part of the brain called the hypothalamus. This part of the brain is responsible for regulating body temperature, emotional responses, and appetite. The hypothalamus produces the main hormones for the body, and also sets our internal biological clock.

For this magnificent hormone regulator to work correctly, it needs the right light signals to be sent to it at the right time. What our ancestors saw as a signal to be relaxed or alert—to hunt and survive—is something quite different today. You can do the same activities today, regardless of whether it is daytime or not.

This is, however, inconvenient because if your sleep is disturbed or intermittent, your hypothalamus will not work correctly since it receives light signals sporadically or at any time. That is why sleep is so crucial to not living in a constant loop of exhaustion during the day and insomnia at night.

Our ancestors slept much better. Before the current advances in technology, their bodies and minds were in sync with the rising and setting of the sun.

Living according to the lapses of sunlight and darkness was undoubtedly something the human body appreciated. So, when the retinas detected the darkness was coming, the pineal gland began to stimulate itself by producing melatonin, the well-known sleep hormone. In the past, this hormone remained in the bloodstream longer, which undoubtedly allowed people to fall asleep better and sleep for more hours.

Modernity and progress produced cities full of light where the night is another dawn of light. Neon lights and shopping centers full of LED illuminate up cities that refuse to sleep. Our homes have also been invaded by the same resplendent vitality until the early morning, and some lights never even go out.

Technological insomnia is a new disease—a consequence of these changes introduced in the life of human beings in the 21st century. It is gaining more and more ground in a world where screens have become essential. Unfortunately, the blue light characteristic of these devices significantly disturbs the human biological clock and wake cycles.

We go to bed and think about taking one last look at our cell phones. Then, we notice a link in our favorite social network that takes us to a video, then to another. We do not realize it, but we can spend an hour surfing the net, maybe two. Cell phones, laptops, and TVs distract us from sleep. We assume we can reach a relaxed state this way, but in reality, the impact these screens have on our brain is enormous.

Most people do not associate this habit with insomnia. "Can a simple look at the mobile or watching some videos hinder my rest?" Absolutely, yes. An activity that is repeated night after night becomes a habit. Furthermore, if we think about it, our retinas are exposed to artificial light. So, we cannot imagine the damage this habit is having, not only on our brains, but on our entire bodies.

According to a study published in *LiveScience*, these kinds of light stimuli disrupt our circadian rhythms completely, in which the word *circadian* translates to "around a day." These rhythms regulate the changes at physical and mental levels that occur over a day. So, if this rhythm is altered, all the functions of the organism are altered, too. That is, the mind will become more and more confused about when it is daytime and when it is night.

EFFECTS OF SCREENS ON OUR BRAINS.

Our screens are now our torches and our magical channels that connect us. Here are the most harmful consequences of this:

As we've already mentioned, the light placed directly on our eyes affects the pineal gland. It interrupts the secretion of melatonin so that our ancestral brain is unable to detect that night has come.

It is common to be in a room with the light off in front of the computer, mobile, or tablet screen. This generates responses at the brain level, since we over-activate many of its structures and enter a state of alertness. This state takes an hour or two to disappear after the devices are turned off. So, if we had six or seven hours to sleep, now we have five hours or less.

Although this new habit is more common among adolescents, more and more adults are complaining of not being able to sleep because they cannot put down their mobile phones. In the youngest, it is the cause of chronic insomnia, physical, and mental fatigue, concentration problems, poor school performance, headaches, and mood swings.[2]

Everything indicates that technological insomnia is going to increase in the coming decades. Since childhood, young people have had access to mobile devices and tablets, and most of the time, they go to bed without family supervision.

So, is the solution to take access to mobile phones and electronic devices away from children? It is not that easy. Above all, it is necessary to be aware of what this addiction entails. Parents should do their best to teach their children better habits and optimize communication. By this, I mean we must understand once and for all that mobile phones cannot be our children's nannies. The solution is intrinsically linked to having wise control over the indiscriminate use of technological devices from the earliest age.

HOW CAN WE REDUCE THE TECHNOLOGICAL IMPACT ON OUR REST AND DAILY LIFE?

- Moderate the light on the screens when bedtime approaches. Both tablets and mobiles now have a "night mode" option, where the impact of blue light is reduced.

---

2 https://hms.harvard.edu/news/screen-time-brain

- Buy blue light filtering glasses. This minimizes the amount of light that enters the retina, which will cause the pineal gland to naturally produce melatonin, thus allowing the person will to feel sleepy.

- At night, we should make use of dimmer lamps and lights. LED light points, although more efficient, also have a stimulating impact on our brain. It is advisable to cover them, at least overnight.

I never tire of emphasizing that a good and healthy rest is important, both in children and adults. The ideal would be to get away from all kinds of technology for at least two hours before going to bed. Replacing your routine of checking your cell phone with reading a book, having a hot cup of tea, or simply having a pleasant conversation is all you need for your brain to relax and get proper rest. In a short time, you will notice that you wake up with the energy to face the new day's challenges.

Chapter 5

All the theories about sleep point it out: Sleep problems can be dangerous to your health and well-being.

The first thing I found in my research is that the need human beings experience to sleep during the day is still an enigma for scientists. Why do conditions such as anxiety, depression, and physical/mental illness often have their roots in sleep deprivation? I will share the most essential theories formulated to answer this question:

INACTIVITY THEORY

Inactivity theory, also called adaptive or evolutionary theory, proposes that the stop to nocturnal activities in humans is an adaptation that works for survival by keeping them out of dangerous areas in times of risk. It is believed that this behavior started in animals. Those who chose to move away and remain still managed to survive, and it led to what we now call sleep.

CONSERVATION OF ENERGY THEORY

Our ancestors faced natural selection—the need to find resources and use them efficiently. This theory is based on the fact that these individuals had to reduce energy expenditure during the night or the day, especially when getting food was unlikely.

RESTORATIVE THEORY

This theory has gained the support of most scientists due to empirical evidence collected through experiments with both human and animal subjects. It is based on the fact that the body needs to restore the energies it uses when awake so that sleep allows the body to repair and rejuvenate itself. Specialists have tested this theory in animals that, being deprived of sleep, lose their immune function and die irretrievably.

This theory states that not only are the body's biological functions repowered during sleep, but the brain and cognitive functions also regenerate cells during sleep.

BRAIN PLASTICITY

This theory is the most recent and is based on the notion that sleep and the brain are related to the changes occurring in the brain. That is why babies usually sleep for many hours. Their brain is getting organized, and they need to be at rest for it do successfully do so. When adults are insomniacs or their rest period is irregular, their cognitive capacity decreases, making them slow, forgetful, and moody.

That being said, all theories mentioned complement each other. The important thing is to understand that either by evolution, survival, or saving energy, all these theories have led scientists to better understand why we feel sleepy. Also, we have more knowledge today about sleep deprivation—something that can negatively affect our bodies.

THE IMPORTANCE OF SLEEP.

Stimulates the immune system
In a state of rest, the body produces a protein called cytokine, which is responsible for attacking infections and inflammation. That means that if we sleep little, our immune system weakens, making us more vulnerable to viruses or bacteria because our defenses drop considerably.

The metabolism is affected.
According to recent studies, obesity has been linked to poor sleep quality and habits. Narcoleptic people tend to be overweight. And not only that, but people who suffer from sleepwalking and insomniacs tend to eat food at dawn. This causes them to gain weight, generating digestive and health disorders that can be avoided if they were to control their sleep cycle.

The cardiovascular system is affected.
In recent research, medical specialists concluded that poor sleep increases the probability of having a cardiovascular issue. This idea is based on the notion that, in this current era of digital technological advances, we have subtracted two hours from our typical hours of sleep. This means that the average rest time has been reduced to five or six hours, on average, And although this varies from person to person, it takes a minimum of eight hours for the body to make all the necessary restorations it needs to, and develop optimal physical and mental functioning.

Additionally, people who do not sleep well are at risk of developing health problems, such as diabetes, hypertension, and obesity, just to name a few.

From a cognitive point of view, not getting enough hours of sleep causes stress. The release of hormones, such as cortisol, is activated to create extra energy that allows a person to fight or flee in instances of danger. This is a healthy response of the endocrine system, controlled by the central nervous system, thus influencing the sleep cycle. Sleeping poorly or little will create a cycle in which a person experiences more stress with high cortisol levels, which ends up worsening stress levels in general.

Memory loss.
During sleep, your body rests, but your brain is awake. It is processing the events of the day and forming memories. Research has revealed that sleep is necessary for the consolidation of memories. Without adequate sleep, your brain will develop an impaired memory and have a hard time absorbing and retaining new information.

Analyzing all this, it is clear how important sleep is for all living beings. It helps us heal physically, recover from illness, de-stress, resolve conflicts, build memories, and optimize our motor skills. And the number of hours you spend in bed does not automatically translate to good sleep. The quality of your rest matters, too.

Inactive brain.
When the brain is tired from days—maybe weeks—of poor sleep, it slows down noticeably. People who sleep less or poorly show signs of mental dullness; they are prone to making more mistakes than those who sleep well. These people will not be attentive during the day. They will find it difficult to

think quickly. This lack of concentration can carry serious consequences if the individual works as a driver, pilot, or cook.

It is not surprising that, cognitively, people with insomnia find it difficult to achieve goals and spend all day with their minds spinning on how to do things. They know they have to do something, but they don't know how or where to start. If you want to achieve goals and be successful, I recommend revisiting Chapter 2, where I provide tips on how to reprogram your mind after you have been able to control your sleep, and how to do it correctly.

Sleeping just a few hours and with interruptions brings serious consequences to one's health. The functions of the organism end up altered, and life expectancy decreases. In the youngest, if they stay awake with their cell phones or tablets until midnight and beyond, some deficiencies in academic performance appears. And in adults, this manifests itself in the work or social field with irritability and lack of attention. There are even work accidents where those involved have later confessed to having had a bad night.

There is an important point that I would like you to understand. The hours of sleep you get cannot be recovered with daytime naps, since the brain does not perform its functions correctly when you sleep during the day. On the contrary, this could affect the stages of sleep and aggravate particular disorders.

Insomnia is the disorder that most frequently reaches medical consultations worldwide. In fact, and according to

WHO statistics, this disease affects at least 30% of people globally.

LACK OF SLEEP CAN TRIGGER ALZHEIMER'S AND EARLY DEMENTIA.

Studies supporting this statement were presented at the Alzheimer's Association International Conference in Vancouver, Canada. These investigations were carried out at The Brigham Hospital in Boston, United States. One of the conclusions reached was that sleep difficulties, including excessive sleeping, too little sleep, and the number of naps a person takes during the day, increase the risk of Alzheimer's and dementia.

The results also showed that those who slept a few hours (less than five) and those who slept eight hours or more had lower average cognitive functions than those who slept seven hours a day. The individuals who participated underwent blood tests to estimate compounds that indicate the onset of Alzheimer's. Those who slept too little or too much showed these changes.

So, sleeping too little or too much should raise a flag in people with sleep disorders, especially older adults.

The key here is anticipation. Sleep difficulties should be addressed early, whether it is too much or too little sleep. The best is to strike a balance. It is recommended to sleep at least seven hours in a row, and if you feel sleepy in the afternoon, take short naps of a maximum of 30 minutes and then stay active until bedtime.

Chapter 6

A healthy rest unleashes your creativity, and you have the power to grow.

We have already discussed what happens when we don't rest properly. It affects us on all levels. More and more specialists agree that taking the necessary time to relax and rest increases levels of creativity. This is because it allows us to tune our mind to the task we are performing and, consequently, make other ideas flourish in those moments of abstraction. The idea that optimal productivity is achieved only in the hours dedicated to work is erroneous. This type of philosophy has created a generation of people overwhelmed by the constant effort to reach increasingly demanding goals and ends up causing an effect opposite to that which is desired.

The capacity for creativity, and therefore innovation, is blocked.

WHAT IS CREATIVITY, AND WHY IS IT SO IMPORTANT FOR PERSONAL DEVELOPMENT?

Creativity is the ability to generate new ideas and concepts. It is synonymous with original thinking, a typical ability of human cognition.

Creativity is an incredible gift possessed by the human race. As the world changes and evolves, we develop new forms of creativity. Many people think they have no creative capacity, but I believe that all human beings are born with this ability. This is because human intelligence is profound and particularly creative. We begin to change everything around us only with our presence, and this is the essence of creating: changing the world we live in.

Our world is a world of ideas, beliefs, and values of imagination and culture. Creativity is not about feeling the world as it is but rather about having ideas about it.

We can even observe the ways in which different communities around the world live according to ideas rooted in their culture, their idiosyncrasy, and their lived experiences.

The great revolutions have been the result of innovative ideas, different ways of seeing the reality that ended up changing the old cultures, which is the fundamental process of change.

Original ideas are mental processes that derive from imagination. Imagination is a private process of the individual—of his inner self. What we imagine in private may have no consequence for the world and may never be known by anyone but ourselves. Creativity is imagination materialized.

We all have imagination, and we have seen it realized more than once. This book, for example, started as an idea in my mind, my imagination, and today, you are reading it. It became something tangible—something that transcended from my mind into your hands.

The creative process

Only human beings have the so-called joint skill: the ability to share worlds and a common focus of attention. The power of symbolic thinking is one of the greatest abilities of human beings, just like language. From infancy, we learn sounds, words, and letters, understanding how they represent concepts. Animals have only a limited capacity for this.

Such symbolic representations have given rise to intricate forms of language: mathematical calculations from Pharaohs' times, music from medieval times, written music (although we know it originated much earlier), and cave art from distant times, to name a few, all of which define our ideas and feelings about the world.

The way our sensory perception perceives the world is unique from person to person because we have different points of view and live in different places.

We have already stated that our ideas or beliefs can liberate or sink us. By literally creating the world we live in, we can also destroy it. In the long cycle of the evolutionary processes of culture throughout history, we find shorter cycles as the creative work of the individual or a group of individuals.

These individual mini-periods of evolutionary change span a lifetime—no more and no less. Throughout life, a person can have one or several creative periods, being able to carry out ideas that are born in one's imagination. These ideas will contribute to changing either that person or their environment.

Creativity improves our emotions.

We can express our personal and social development, as well as our feelings, through art. For those who think it is something complicated, I tell them they do not have to be an expert in the subject or have deep knowledge in it. We are all perfectly capable of being creative.

Whoever uses imagination improves an emotional condition. Having expressed our feelings and emotions through the various creative currents, we will feel confident and secure. The most notable benefit is it has a direct impact on self-esteem. It stimulates it and positions it high, which is where everyone should aim for their self-esteem to be.

Originality is often confused with something that no one in the world has ever seen, but common sense tells us that something creative can be original on different levels, for the individual, the community, or humanity. When we find our vocation, we discover the true power of creativity and start offering the best personal creative talents we can have.

Being creative is an undeniable advantage.

Every culture brings new ideas and concepts to gain a sense of belonging and purpose. Success comes from understanding your contribution to the world, and the spark of this contribution comes from a creative place. Understanding the power that comes from creativity can help elevate us in many ways.

Creativity is the joy of living, which is to experiment, innovate, take risks, break rules, make mistakes, and learn from them. This state of joy that starts by following our creative instincts gives us meaning and purpose, helps us build our humanity, and exponentially increases our ability to succeed.

Creativity is increasingly important in the connected economy nowadays because it delivers the best outcome. As the world continues its race toward innovation, faster and cheaper are synonymous with what sets us apart from the crowd in terms of individual creative contribution. The more we share and create, the more we discover how valuable this concept is.

Below, I describe four ways creativity leads to a more successful life:

1. Creativity creates a deeper connection to work.
Creativity is the act of experimenting and learning about what works and does not work. When we see creativity as part of our work and not something left to a small artistic elite, we can establish a deeper connection to the work we do in the world. If we see our job as part of a larger purpose, our success will increase every time we demonstrate creativity.

The more you can see, understand, and feel a creative imprint, the bigger impact it will have. If you see an opportunity to think outside the box in a particular situation because you see the world differently than your peers, then you have the advantage of providing value that no one else can. And guess what? Each of us sees the world differently, as part of our uniqueness.

You already possess that special edge, even if you were not sure of it before. It is intimidating to come forward with ideas that may be the object of jokes from the people around us. That is why many people constantly avoid sharing their creative thoughts, resist their inner talents, and hide from the possibilities regarding their creativity.

The self-confidence they need comes from knowing that what they show to the world is unique and can fully identify them, even if they are mixed in a crowd.

2. Ask the question

One of the ways you can increase the ability to bring creativity into your life is having a "what if?" mindset. Spending quality time wondering, dreaming, and not stressing about the consequences of being wrong can be liberating.

If what we created was not judged or had no real consequences beyond an act of wonder, we could imagine new solutions to old problems. Elon Musk is a good example of the "what if?" approach. He applied it when he created a company with the aim of making commercial space flight possible. His company is not based on what it is, but what it could be.

By incorporating this sense of wonder and fun into our work, life, and worldly contribution, we can let go of some of the self-imposed limits we have placed on our success. If we treat our work and life a little more like a playground, we will see growth in our ability to perform and contribute.

3. Opportunity for new thinking

Sometimes, when we are working on a project, either on a team or alone, we may find that we are hitting a wall searching for a solution to a problem. Instead of looking for the answer, sometimes, we need to allow our creative brain instead to search for answers that may be hidden. And by hidden, I mean not yet created.

Take some time to step back from the work at hand and simply consider things that may seem impossible but may generate new ideas. By daring to combine ideas, you can reach a solution that you would not otherwise see.

For example, posing a question and simply wondering about a solution might generate a solution you did not see in the first place. For instance, how could we improve the passenger boarding process at the airport by envisioning new ideas that did not exist before?

4. Create new avenues of learning and increase brain activity. When we are creative, we begin to open our minds to new thoughts. We begin to see new ideas and opportunities that we did not notice before. We also silence our amygdala or our "lizard brain," which is often in fight or flight mode to protect us.

I will discuss = visualization extensively in a future chapter because I am sure that, along with creativity, it will give you the tools to achieve the success you so desire.

Chapter 7

The sleep pattern in the golden years.

Age is an aggravating factor of insomnia because as the years go by, we sleep less. I remember when I was a teenager, I could sleep on top of a rock. As the years went by, this quality diminished. Nighttime wakefulness at this age is directly related to sleep interruptions (we need to go to the bathroom frequently) and symptoms caused by chronic diseases. Many people agree that the older they get, the lighter their sleep is.

RETIREMENT AFFECTS QUALITY OF REST.

As retirement draws near, people are filled with anticipation about what their life will be like when they can finally enjoy their golden years. But nothing prepares them for a sudden change in their daily activities. The routine and dynamic they have implemented for years changes, stress and physical activity decrease, and sleep is affected.

Most retirees have reported sleep deprivation as the most visible and immediate change in their lifestyle once they retired. The first few months can be very frustrating, in which many aimlessly wander around the house late at night without because they cannot sleep.

The time a newly retired person wakes up can vary wildly at this stage. It no longer depends on an alarm, and that is why the body gradually finds its own rhythm. I have already mentioned that physical activity and exercise are a great help in falling asleep. Therefore, a simple night walk can be quite helpful at this stage.

BENEFICIAL TIPS TO APPLY AT THE BEGINNING OF YOUR RETIREMENT

Stay calm

Knowing that you are only going through an adjustment stage and insomnia will not stay forever is comforting. Many people start taking sleeping pills out of desperation. The wisest thing to do is wait for your sleep pattern to balance out naturally.

Make Plans

All those expectations you've always had for your retirement are often put on hold indefinitely. The confinement of the last two years has numbed us on a social level, but as humanity moves forward and overcomes the pandemic, it is time to return to normal.

Organize meetings and activities with your fellow retirees. Engage with fewer WhatsApp groups and Zoom sessions and schedule more in-person meetings, of course, observing health measures at all times.

Continue the good sleep habits I describe in Chapter 3. Avoid the use of your cell phone beyond bedtime, as tempting as it may be. I will talk in-depth about what technological insomnia means in the 21st century in a later chapter.

Every stage in life is full of meaning.

Each stage of life must be full of purpose. While it is true that climbing the Himalayas is an unrealistic goal for most seniors, it is important to engage in meaningful activities. With plenty of free time, you can afford to try new things, visit museums, and go birdwatching in the city park. These activities should not only be adopted to fill a vacant space in our retirement schedule, but must also be activities in which we identify with and thoroughly enjoy. They should feed our soul, which will lead us to fall asleep at the end of the day with a smile on our faces.

WHAT ARE YOUR OPTIONS WHEN YOU TRY TO MITIGATE INSOMNIA?

When we are dealing with a lack of sleep, we want an immediate solution. The most common solutions range from sleep-inducing herbs in less severe cases, to drug therapy. Lack of sleep leads many individuals to try to solve the problem for themselves. They will likely go to a specialist after weeks of trying various alternatives.

Usually, the first option is to take herbal teas, such as valerian. Although they may help, these natural sedatives are mild and are not as effective in cases of severe insomnia. Taking melatonin supplement caps is also very popular, and studies indicate that regular use is quite safe. Side effects may include headaches, nausea, and daytime drowsiness.

Drugs

Several drugs are currently available, and they intervene in different ways at the cellular level to obtain a stable sleep pattern. But along with the benefit each of them can bring, there are several adverse effects, such as headaches, daytime drowsiness, and even respiratory problems. Not to mention, of course, the dreaded dependence.

The risk is bigger for the elderly, as they likely already have a daily intake of medications for chronic conditions that can produce a reaction when taken with sleeping medications.

There are no hard and fast rules when it comes to healing insomnia, and all organisms have unique characteristics and backgrounds. The success of a determined therapy requires a previous study of the patient's conditions.

There are cases of severe insomnia in which medications and a simple change of habits are not an option. These patients are often in a state of permanent distress. On the one hand, they feel the consequences of not getting enough rest. On the other hand, they are in a state of constant distress about not falling asleep and have an understandable concern related to deteriorating health.

Sleeping pills can provide immediate relief, but they are addictive. Over time, regular doses no longer have the effect they had in the beginning.

These people have tried everything. They have arranged to improve their sleep environment and even observed some or all of the good practices in Chapter 3, but still, their insomnia persists. What are the options for them?

CBT-I. Cognitive-behavioral therapy applied to insomnia. Extensive research on the topic has developed a short-term therapy that has proven effective in the most difficult cases related to insomnia.

What is CBT-I

This therapy[3] seeks a radical change in sleep patterns using several techniques that do not involve drugs and are designed for long-term improvement. The duration is six to eight sessions to start noticing results, although some patients have achieved positive results much earlier.

If the person has been taking drugs to help them sleep, the therapist will take note, and the first session will most likely consist of an interview in which the patient's sleep history is analyzed to create a customized treatment plan.

There is no limitation to access this therapy, and its success has been demonstrated in adolescents, adults, and the elderly.

This multiple action treatment intervenes in:

1. ***The area of cognitive development of the individual***, using techniques aimed at transforming the patient's mindset by dismantling negative beliefs related to sleep. During these sessions, most of the beliefs linked to anxiety and depression are attacked.

---

3 https://www.sleepfoundation.org/insomnia/treatment/cognitive-behavioral-therapy-insomnia

2. ***Stimulus control.*** During therapy, the patient should be in bed only if asleep or having sex. As a general rule, you should not be awake in bed for more than ten minutes. To achieve this, scheduled alarms are set. The therapist must closely monitor this intentional sleep limitation. By reducing time in bed, a state of tiredness during the day appears, and eventually, it will manifest more often at bedtime. If therapy is working, the patient will obtain more sleep as the therapy progresses.

3. ***Relaxation Techniques.*** They are intended to achieve a state of both mental and physical relaxation: meditation, breathing exercises, and hypnosis sessions (this topic is extensively discussed in Chapter 8) are often combined.

4. ***Biofeedback.*** It consists of monitoring the processes in our body using technology for this purpose. These readings (temperature, heart rate, brain waves), will give us invaluable data to learn how our body works and how it influences our rest.

Optimization of the bedroom environment.
In Chapter 3, we talked about a particular improvement that helps us create the necessary conditions for uninterrupted rest.

Review and correction of bad sleeping habits.
You can think of this as a cleanse, identifying each habit that contributes to our insomnia, then replacing it with proper sleep practices (Chapter 3). You may already be implementing various related techniques. It is best to share this information with your therapist. The ultimate goal, remember, is to design a unique treatment for your case.

Stage of education at the psychological level.

At this stage, we continue to increase good habits. thus reinforcing the connection between thoughts, emotions, and good sleep.

CBT-I is a type of therapy that analyzes the unique conditions of each individual and acts based on this important data to provide a completely personalized treatment. And by integrating these new habits into our daily lives, a general mental transformation takes place that will positively affect other areas of our lives.

Although the effects of this therapy are not as immediate as those involving medication, they still tend to last longer because CBT-I is a replacement of habits and beliefs aimed at permanent improvement.

The best dreams

happen

When you are

awake

Chapter 8

The power of hypnotherapy.

Far away is the image people used to have about hypnosis: a man with a pendulum trying to trap the patient's mind, seeking to enter his subconscious and manage it at will. Far from television shows full of lies and exaggeration is the truth:

It is a wonderful therapeutic tool the psychologist or specialist can use, along with other techniques, within a treatment plan for a patient. With it, the therapist guides the patient while constructing situations as if they were real. Thus, if everything goes well, the person behaves accordingly. After, the therapist draws conclusions based on the behavior of this individual under hypnosis. It is a treatment that has helped millions of people with internal conflicts and conditions like phobias, psychosis, or unexplained depression.

MYTHS ABOUT HYPNOSIS

The main myth about this therapy—thanks to unscrupulous charlatans—is that many people see it as an irrational phenomenon closer to the paranormal than to truthful science.

The person subjected to hypnosis loses total control of his consciousness.

If the person loses consciousness, it is because he or she falls asleep. For that reason, the professional in charge will not be able to continue the therapy, since the active participation of the person still in the hypnosis state is essential for the therapy's success.

The hypnotist possesses strange powers.
The therapist possesses knowledge based on the science regarding psychology, and therapeutic skills to treat certain disorders that otherwise have been impossible to cure.

Under hypnosis, no one can lie.
This assumption is completely false. Under hypnosis, the information revealed is only that which the person's subconscious allows. The patient never ceases to have control.

The hypnotist can make us perform any action he wants us to perform.
Not at all. The subject is guided by the therapist until a certain limit. The patient goes only where the patient wants to go and not beyond. Additionally, many have the belief that we will lose all control over our behavior, but in reality, we would not be hypnotized if we did not want to be. We can emerge from the state of hypnosis whenever we choose.

Hypnosis is not based on having passive subjects. The patient has to be well aware of his or her actions, using imagination, which leads to becoming emotionally involved in the treatment.

Myths engender fear and act as though they can take us away from that which could benefit us or bring us closer to that which could harm us. All the fears and misgivings about hypnosis are unfounded. I have already explained that during a hypnosis session, the person does not become an automaton. Therefore, the patient will not perform acts he or she does not agree with. These beliefs are typical of fiction movies.

The reality is different. Hypnotherapy is a beneficial practice, as long as it is performed by a certified and experienced therapist.

There is no doubt that hypnotherapy is a technique of suggestion. It has been widely studied, and its validity has been proven in many fields of psychological medicine. Even so, I must emphasize that the guarantee of its effectiveness will depend on a series of features of the patient's personality: his or her capacity for imagination, response to previous therapies, whether the person has any degenerative memory disease, and so on.

Once the therapist is sure of everything, they recommend engaging in a testing session where the therapist induces the patient to relax and let go, focusing on the suggested words and images. It is extremely important to maintain an open attitude to the suggestions regarding the positive transformation of thoughts, emotions, and behaviors.

DIFFERENT TYPES OF HYPNOSIS

1 Traditional hypnosis (by suggestion)
Traditional hypnosis is based on the induction of a trance state; once the person being treated reaches this state, he or she will

receive verbal suggestions regarding his or her behavior or mental contents. The main goal of this method is to predispose the subconscious, for example, by recommending that the person abandon a negative habit or belief.

2. Ericksonian hypnosis

Milton H. Erickson, an American psychologist, was responsible for developing this type of hypnosis. He has been considered a pioneer in this field and others in psychotherapy. This therapy does not use direct suggestions, but rather offers the patient comparisons that urge him to have more creative thinking and reflect on the problems at hands, thinking of ways to deal with them. It is a gentle method of suggestion ideal for people who are apprehensive about the hypnotherapy procedure.

3. Cognitive-behavioral hypnosis

This method tries to modify significant changes in behavior through suggestions. The influence on the patient is explained as a consequence of the interaction of the patient's mind, physical relaxation, the use of imagination, and the person's intentions or beliefs.

Some therapists who ascribe to the cognitive-behavioral orientation use hypnosis techniques as a complement to broader interventions, such as sleep-wake disturbances, addictions, or erratic personality behaviors.

4. Self-hypnosis

We speak of self-hypnosis when a person induces this state through autosuggestion. When we go to social networks, we encounter thousands of videos and audios that can induce deep relaxation. However, this is only useful for simple situations. For instance, these are usually used to develop intrapersonal and interpersonal skills (such as assertiveness), induce relaxation and reduce the level of stress, face stage fright, lose weight, or quit smoking. For deeper problems, the guidance of a professional therapist is required.

5. Neurolinguistics Programming (NLP)

Although I cannot say that it is strictly a type of hypnosis, neuro-linguistic programming or NLP is closely related to these methods. This technique. created by Richard Bandler and John Grinder, uses "thought patterns" to optimize psychological skills.

How does the hypnotic trance occur?

The hypnotic experience can be summarized as certain sensory experiences where the therapist's or hypnotist's suggestions lead the subject to relax and focus on the most intimate experiences, thoughts, sensations, and emotions. It is simply an interaction between two people in which the patient is directed through his or her attention. It can be broad, but blurry, or erratic without order or direction. It is the therapist's job to lead the session in the best possible way to obtain information that can benefit the patient.

As I have already mentioned, leading a person through hypnosis is done through suggestions, which have three fundamental characteristics:

- Make them in such a way that they surpass the critical observations of the subject's conscious mind.

- The suggestions must be well-structured so that they are understandable.

- The content must unequivocally address the subject to the objective sought.

EXAMPLE OF HYPNOSIS INDUCTION.

At first, the patient keeps his hands about 20 to 30 cm apart. It is a clue as to how the subconscious manifests itself. If the unconscious wants to be induced, then the hands will come together. On the contrary, if the hands remain separated, the person is not ready. If they come together after a few minutes of relaxation, it means the subject is subconsciously ready to enter a hypnotic trance.

With this simple body language, the hypnotist establishes a method for the patient's unconscious to relate to the conscious. If the hands are separated, it means he does not like the task. If the hands are close, he agrees with the task.

At this point in the session, the therapist, noticing the position of the patient's hands, offers the therapeutic suggestions he considers necessary and ensures they coincide with the exhalations of the subject in trance.

THE THERAPIST'S JOB DURING HYPNOSIS.

The therapist's job is to use precise and consistent language, paying attention to the sensitivity of the subject's mood changes to support the necessary therapeutic results.

The therapist is responsible for recognizing and giving the patient the necessary space to spontaneously interpret the changes he or she is experiencing in real time. That will allow the person to more deeply understand the origin of the problems.

The therapist must properly communicate, so the patient is aware his or her unconscious is in control.

FACTORS THAT CAN INFLUENCE THE DEGREE OF SUGGESTIBILITY OF THE PATIENT.

- The person's expectations, beliefs, motivation, abilities, imagination, and so on.

- The therapist's communicative style, how he or she carries out the hypnotic procedures, and the management of the patient's resistance, among others.

- Communication and trust are fundamental to determining whether the relationship is good or bad. That is important in the bonding between therapist and patient.

In hypnotic sessions, the experiences can feel quite real. It is the result of good suggestibility work. The patient expresses them as if he or she was watching a movie while paying full attention to the suggested scenes and processing them as if they were real. This outcome is possible because there is an excellent degree of suggestion made by the therapist.

BENEFITS OF HYPNOTHERAPY

Hypnosis is beneficial for both physical (medical) and psychological problems.

It is effective in relieving physical pain, such as migraines and fibromyalgia, and is used to reduce the negative symptoms of chemotherapy, such as nausea, in cancer patients. Insomnia and anxiety cases have been reduced after the use of hypnotherapy.

It has even treated patients after traumatic experiences, giving very encouraging results for those involved. During maternity, many women resort to hypnosis to improve symptoms such as nausea, back pain, and swelling, while also reducing pain at the time of childbirth. Hypnotherapeutic sessions can also be useful in learning to give up habits, such as giving up tobacco and alcohol. It is important that the person is determined to accept the change since he or she will have to work on the habit's eradication, face the anxiety, and fight against the effects of abstinence.

Hypnosis does not ensure magical or immediate answers but requires a commitment from the patient to make the behavioral change real and effective.

I can affirm that hypnosis is a beneficial technique for certain physical and psychological problems because it directly deals with more than 80% of them originating in the subconscious mind. The studies and investigations do not stop to demonstrate the effectiveness of this branch of the therapy. I have been a great student of this wonderful therapeutic tool and recommend it extensively.

Chapter 9

Benefits of Meditation for True Relaxation.

Evidence of meditation practice has been found in ancient civilizations. The earliest records of its use date back to 1500 BC. In the West, interest in Buddhism began around the 18th century. The English publication of the Tibetan *Book of the Dead* in 1927 allowed people to understand the mysteries of death and how to attain enlightenment. These practices became popular among writers and the nobility of the time.

The bigger growth of meditation practice in the West occurred from the 18th century onward when interest in Buddhism increased. Hermann Hesse, the German writer and author of *Siddhartha*, the book recounting a spiritual journey of self-discovery, gave the reader a glimpse into meditation beyond the religious aspect, emphasizing stress reduction, relaxation, and self-improvement, which could be obtained from this practice.

The information about meditation is quite extensive nowadays. Although meditation is a novelty that likely came from the East, it is now a common habit for many people on this side of the world. This is due to the multiple advantages that this knowledge offers; the close relationship between body-mind-meditation is no longer a privilege that only a few know.

I am pleased to talk about it since I began searching for answers in this millenary experience some years ago, which led me to study with the best, among them, the master, Eckhard Wunderle, at the Institut für Spirituelle Psychologie.

Through these pages, I will transmit to you the most important points that I learned about why and how to meditate, why it works, and the changes that meditation causes to the brain and the whole organism if we practice it with constancy.

THE INCREDIBLE BENEFITS OF MEDITATION WILL IMPROVE YOUR REST.

The effects that meditation has on the human body are scientifically proven. Meditation stimulates the creation of hormones essential for the proper chemical functioning of our body.

Recall the sleep hormone, melatonin. How are melatonin and meditation related?

Meditation undoubtedly contributes to increased energy and peace of mind. The research conducted both scientifically and psychologically has shown that the regular practice of meditation generates an increase in melatonin levels in people who perform the activity.

This hormone is responsible for the regulation and quality of sleep. Melatonin is produced by the amino acid tryptophan.

This essential amino acid is generated in the pineal gland, known for hundreds of years as "the seat of the soul."

Eastern traditions directed the flow of meditation towards this gland. They believed that by unblocking the pineal gland, many blockages in the body causing diseases and ailments would be released.

Countless studies on the effects of meditation and the improvement of sleep have been carried out, and I have seen how meditation works wonders in this regard:

- People who practice meditation for 30 nights in a row had better sleep compared to when they did not meditate.
- These people expressed that they achieved more continuous hours of sleep.
- They also said that when they woke up, they felt more energetic and in a better mood. This was not the case before meditation practice.

HOW DOES IT WORK?

A research team at the University of Massachusetts investigated the relationship between melatonin and meditation in 1995. These studies yielded some fascinating data about the meditation-melatonin link.

Meditation helps regulate the adrenal pituitary hypothalamus responsible for cortisol, aldosterone, adrenaline, and noradrenaline levels. They also produce sex hormones (estrogen and testosterone).

Melatonin has a sleep-inducing effect on the individual through inhibition of the suprachiasmatic nucleus, as well as acting as an antioxidant and immunomodulator.[4] In addition to being an important antioxidant, melatonin generates a pleasant sensation of well-being.

Concentration also improves notably by regulating the hormones in the body. The person gets better rest, and more hours of deep sleep, thus making miracles in the cognitive faculties of the individual.

Through meditation, the mechanisms that generate sleep can be modified. It is undoubtedly an ally to improve health through rest. Meditation also opens a wide field of debate to understand the mechanisms of human consciousness.

Meditation and success
The benefits of meditation are many. This practice or philosophy of life produces modifications in brain regions related to memory, self-awareness, empathy, and stress. So, apart from being seen as something with mere spirituality, it truly modifies the physical and mental health of those who cultivate it as part of their daily life.

A group of researchers from the Massachusetts General Hospital published the results of studies on the benefits of meditation in the journal, *Psychiatric Research*. They affirm that after eight weeks of daily meditations, the participants presented brain modifications, such as an increase in the gray

---

4　https://www.sciencedirect.com/science/article/abs/pii/0306987795902996

matter of the hippocampus (memory) and other areas related to self-awareness, compassion, and introspection.

In fact, when you meditate, you feel better because your mind relaxes. This is because the structure of your brain has properly modified its connections. The good news is, you do not need to be a meditation expert to reap its benefits. Anyone can access minutes of relaxation and mindfulness and feel how their capacity for emotional integration increases and how their cognitive faculties begin to positively expand.

Therefore, you can see that meditation frees thoughts, making you focus on the present, while also overcoming stress and worries. Is this not the way to a better life? Is this not the way to a more stable life where your mind is there to make your life better, not worse?

Benefits of meditation
- ✓ Helps to rest and relax our mind.
- ✓ Reduces blood pressure.
- ✓ Significantly expands the memory.
- ✓ Improves emotional stability.
- ✓ Contributes to greater personal awareness.
- ✓ Facilitates and improves sleep quality.
- ✓ Improves overall health.
- ✓ Relaxes muscular tension.
- ✓ Increases the power of concentration.
- ✓ It favors the improvement of the mood.

HOW CAN YOU MEDITATE?

Basic meditation should begin in a quiet place where you are not interrupted. You can wear comfortable clothes and sit or lie down. Begin by breathing deeply, holding the air in for at least five seconds, and exhaling slowly while concentrating on your every breath. Relax your mind and keep focused so you can move away from your regular thoughts, at least for a few minutes.

If your activities and lifestyle do not allow you the necessary time to do this, you can meditate at any time and place. Just sit in a comfortable position with your back straight, hands on your knees, and breathe deeply.

You must concentrate on your breathing, focusing on your diaphragm as it rises and falls.

To start, I recommend short sessions of five to ten minutes, and increasing the time as you progress to twenty minutes a day.

Note that medication also helps strengthen emotional intelligence. As we all know, emotional intelligence helps us eliminate limiting beliefs, have clarity in our desires, and focus on the here and now.

MEDITATION AND LIMITING BELIEFS

Through meditation, you can eliminate limiting beliefs and overcome irrational fears. When meditating, you must do it with visualizations. If you do not handle this subject well, I recommend you read Chapter 11, where I explain the power of visualizing.

When you are relaxed, imagine the fear and give it a face. It can be a wild animal, a dark forest, or a huge cave. Concentrate on what you feel when you come face to face with your fears, anxiety, anger, or sadness. Reflect on what you feel for a few seconds.

Now, visualize a door or a passage in the forest. There is a shining light there. Go towards it, and as you move, leave behind what you fear, turn your back to that fear, get out of there, and imagine you arrive at a place where you no longer feel that fear. It can be a party you remember, a walk with your pet, or simply visualizing yourself sitting in front of a wonderful place, breathing calmly and giving thanks for having overcome the issue that overwhelms you so much.

You can repeat this meditation/visualization as many times as you deem necessary until you internalize the new belief in your subconscious.

WE ALL HAVE HARD DAYS WHEN WE THINK EVERYTHING IS GOING WRONG

We've all had bad days. I will teach you how to connect with that positive and hopeful side that we all need to overcome a bad day and regain calm:

Start by breathing deeply. If you need relaxing music or soft scented incense, do not hesitate to resort to it. That will make you enter a state of relaxation more easily.

Now, think about that thing that bothers you or that action that messed with your day or week. Think about it just for a moment. Now, move your mind to a happy memory, something in the past that brought you joy. A walk with your parents, a stay at the beach, or your first kiss. In short, resort to a powerful memory that replaces recent events. Focus on that memory. Bring to your mind what you felt, the colors, the smells, and try to remember the textures of what you touched that day. The idea is to retain it as vividly as possible for as long as possible.

Leave it in your mind even after you finish meditating, and observe how you feel. I'm sure the bad day will be at least 90% gone. Next, we just have to open our eyes and focus on the present, the here and now, to feel relaxed.

Now you can think of solutions on what to do so your bad streak does not happen again. I assure you that solutions will come to your mind more clearly after this meditation.

Guided Meditation
In this technology-filled world, many forms of meditation reach the public through social media, video, and audio platforms. Guided meditation is a way to help a person reach maximum concentration and relaxation.

It is mainly based on the presence of a spiritual guide, something I have done countless times to lead beginners to overcome the difficulties of meditation when they are starting.

Mindfulness meditation
This modern kind of meditation emphasizes mindfulness. In a world where we have so many activities going on at once and hardly any time for ourselves, we see life automatically, without

much attention. This branch of meditation teaches us to live in the present moment, in the here and now.

It takes us away from the negative things in our past. It is about living without the anxiety of one uncertain future and being more focused on the present. We concentrate on worthwhile things, enjoying every moment with our full attention.

There is no doubt that with meditation, we will feel more relaxed, but by making it more active, we will be able to overcome limiting beliefs that hinder our path to success. We will also accept ourselves better, leaving aside harmful and repetitive thoughts. Meditating helps us grow internally, and that is not something we should lose.

Better Dreams
My-mindguide.com

Chapter 10

The many advantages of achieving a night of restful sleep.

As you have read throughout this book, sleep is extremely important for health. While you sleep, your mind and body do not shut down overnight. All your internal organs and processes remain working tirelessly. Sleeping correctly during the right amount of hours maintains all the properties of the body in one way or another. The energetic and molecular balance, intellectual functions of the individual, and a state of alertness also facilitate interactions by stimulating good attitude.

A tired person performs poorly in all aspects of their life. There is no doubt that sleep helps you think more clearly, have faster reflexes, and better concentration. I invite you to observe how a person who enjoys a good rest behaves regularly. You will find that this person operates at an optimal level, has better responses to surprise events, is in a better mood, and can easily communicate with anyone in any setting.

As you have already seen, lack of sleep can cause accidents both at work and outside. Insomnia increases the risk of depression and anxiety. Resting well is very important for the brain since rest affects almost all body tissues, hormones, the immune system, appetite, breathing, blood pressure, and cardiovascular health.

Recent studies linking rest to viruses have revealed that sleep can impact the effectiveness of vaccines. It has been stressed that people who slept better had a better response and stronger protection against the disease. Regardless of whether you are pro-vaccine or not, I suggest you consider that not sleeping well affects your immune system, which protects us against any virus.

A beneficial sleep should include four or five sleep cycles. Each cycle includes periods of deep sleep and rapid eye movement (REM) or desynchronized sleep; this is when we dream. As the night progresses, the fraction of that cycle increases in the desynchronized sleep. This pattern of cycles and progression is fundamental to the biology of sleep. That is why it is so harmful not to sleep enough hours, or to wake up several times a night in what is called interrupted sleep. By not completing the complete cycles, the body becomes unbalanced in all aspects.

Each person has a variable sleep need. The average number of hours of sleep required by a young adult is seven to eight continuous hours. Babies and children generally sleep between twelve and sixteen hours a day, and teenagers get between nine and ten hours of sleep—or at least it is what they need to get the restorative benefit of one sleep cycle.

But it is precisely in young people that sleep interruptions are more common due to the exaggerated use of stimulants such as caffeine or soft drinks. Also included are distractions from electronic devices, especially cell phones, tablets, and laptops. All of them conspire to shorten more and more the hours of rest—something extremely dangerous for the health, of which I spoke of extensively in Chapter 4.

Sleep disorders are frequent in the elderly. They are often the consequence of medications, severe depression, and conditions for aging. According to the WHO, in North America alone, more than 70 million people of all ages suffer from chronic sleep problems. That translates into more absences from work and school, which are, in the long run, a considerable waste of time and money.

Among the most common treatments for this disorder and those I have mentioned in previous chapters are relaxation and deep breathing techniques, as well as meditation. Practicing yoga and even visualizations are all therapies I've successfully used on countless patients. The perseverance and commitment of the person in doing the exercises and leading a healthy life are decisive for their recovery.

BENEFITS OF SLEEPING WELL

Cellular regeneration is facilitated.
When we sleep, our skin also rests. Cells tend to regenerate and are more easily oxygenated, specifically in the eyes. Rhodopsin (light-sensitive pigment) recovers from the effort exerted during the day.

Getting a good night's sleep helps maintain healthy weight.

According to studies carried out by nutrition specialists, if our body does not rest enough, it accumulates fat, which later becomes more difficult to burn. Additionally, poor rest causes the body to produce more of the ghrelin hormone, which is responsible for increasing our appetite accumulating abdominal fat.

Lack of rest makes it easier for adipocytes—the fat cells—to release less leptin, the appetite-suppressing hormone. So, little sleep is associated with digestive disorders and obesity.

Lower incidence of disease such as hypertension and diabetes. If we do not get enough rest, we are at risk of contracting diseases such as hypertension or diabetes, which is a result of the increased production of hormones, such as cortisol, also known as the "stress hormone."

A good night's sleep reduces the risks of heart disease.
During sleep, our heart rate also decreases, which helps the recovery work done by coronary cells and tissues. This is where the body releases melatonin, which is as important for sleep as it is for growth.

A recent study published in the *European Heart Journal* states that people who suffer from insomnia are three times more likely to suffer a cardiovascular accident than those who sleep six to eight hours a night. Why? Well, insomnia increases blood levels of stress hormones, blood pressure, and heart rate. It has also been discovered that these patients tend to have high cholesterol, which is a preemptive indicator of heart disease.

Improves your intellectual capacity

Sleeping is essential for developing intellectual capacity. Our brain needs to disconnect for several hours to process all the information accumulated during the day. This process is important to maintain and improve our most basic and most complex cognitive abilities. We speak of the person's ability to make a simple spatial deduction or pattern recognition by linking these skills to mathematical or verbal skills.

Promotes coordination

A psychomotor activity cannot be carried out correctly if our brain is affected by stress and poor sleep. I have known people that, after a night of bad sleep, say they trip over all the furniture in the house. Even so, it is less dangerous than driving in that state.

Sleeping well gives us the brain-extremity coordination necessary to coordinate the mind and body.

Increases creativity.

Creativity is one of the most incredible benefits of a good rest. When our mind has rested and our body is balanced from a hormonal point of view, our memory works perfectly, therefore enhancing levels of creativity. That is because ideas come easily, and we can connect memories and situations that release our ability to create.

You feel healthier.

During this pandemic, the importance of caring for our immune system has gained prominence; it is the shield that protects us against diseases. The body's immune system uses sleep to regenerate itself. If we have a weak and erratic immune system due to sleep problems, we can be exposed to toxins and germs that continually threaten us. That would lead us to have less opportunity to successfully defeat viruses and infections.

Improves memory
Sleep favors the neural connections necessary for memory. During the REM phase of sleep, the hippocampus, the storehouse of our memory, is restored, and short-term memory is transformed into long-term memory. So, if you feel that you forget silly things throughout the day, or have a hard time remembering them, pay attention to your sleep. If you do not sleep well at night, try to take a 30-minute nap. Rest and disconnect for a while, and see how you wake up with a clearer mind.

SLEEP WELL, A CURE FOR DEPRESSION.

As I have repeated in previous chapters, when the body sleeps, it facilitates the production of melatonin and serotonin. These hormones can counteract the effects of hormones that cause stress, such as adrenaline and cortisol. This balance means that we feel happier and emotionally stronger. These two feelings are necessary for people suffering from some level of depression; feeling that they can be themselves again will give them the motivation they need to keep fighting. If they get to sleep the necessary hours to balance their hormonal system, they will come out of this terrible disease.

These are the most immediate benefits of getting a good night's sleep. Feeling good is priceless, and if we make significant effort, whether to improve our diet, engage in low-impact exercises, or abandon our mobile phones before going to bed, we will notice major improvements in our physical and mental health.

Chapter 11

The power of visualization.

A relaxed and rested mind at its maximum potential is powerful. The thoughts and emotions that come from it will have the power to modify your reality. However, this requires perseverance, constant work, and an understanding of the tools that I am going to share in this chapter. My goal is to help you build an ideal present, one you can happily live in.

Positive visualization is the process of constructing images in your mind that represent pleasant or beneficial scenarios. However, it is important that you consider the scene to be as realistic as possible. Engaging your senses will strengthen the idea in your mind, and it is what differentiates creative visualization from contemplative imagination. Your senses are participants in what your mind can see.

Many people find it difficult to successfully visualize themselves. That is due to the erroneous beliefs that they have in their subconscious. But don't worry; these beliefs can also be changed through visualization.

Before I give you those details, you need to understand how your thoughts work so you can master and change them with time.

Our thoughts are based on our beliefs, and these beliefs can be positive or negative. I am not referring to what is good or bad; there are universal understandings. It is good to be positive, happy, and diligent, and it is bad to be negative, pessimistic, and moody. Beliefs are different and unique to each person. Someone wrote that the answers are in the questions. Just ask yourself the right questions about your beliefs, and you'll establish a better understanding of what you stand for and what you value.

Do my beliefs help me be better at what I do? Will it make me happy in my relationship to think this way? Will my thoughts and attitudes help me succeed in life?

Each answer will be different. But no matter where you are now, you can go further by investing your energy in changing those limiting beliefs to positive ones that will make you grow. Creative visualization will help you with these two things:

- Change the beliefs, customs, and even attitudes that are limiting and replace them with constructive ones.
- Change your reality to get a better job, a bigger house, a pleasant trip, and so on.

It is important to stress that this technique will not magically make your dreams real. As I said before, it is a technique that prepares the brain to receive exactly what we imagine. When I refer to creative visualization, I mean it is a scientifically proven cognitive technique that uses the imagination to generate images in our minds that symbolize the goals we want to achieve and thus cause positive changes in our lives.

For the visualization to work, it is good that you consider several points:

- It is not as simple as it seems; it is not enough to just imagine it.
- It is necessary to have an open mind, and as I said before, overcome limiting beliefs.
- You need to forget about fear and limitations and convince yourself that what you are visualizing is possible, otherwise you are wasting your time.

You must be realistic and establish transparent, feasible, and realistic goals.

Your goals must be achievable. It is where common sense takes hold; no matter how many visualizations you engage in about being skinny and weighing in at your goal weight, visualizations alone won't help you if you don't have a diet and exercise plan in place. This means you have to know how to distinguish between attainable dreams and those that are impossible. So, if you combine good sense with positive and realistic visualization, you will be able to achieve everything you want to achieve.

Concrete images.
We have to form vivid and concrete images in our minds. This applies to ideal situations or conversations that we want to achieve. Normally, the mind begins to wander. To stay focused, meditate a few minutes before each visualization exercise.

Repeat the visualization several times.
It is necessary to intentionally conserve and sustain these images in our minds over time. I recommend doing this in

a quiet place, away from distractions. Ideally, you want to do several visualizations a day, each ranging from ten to fifteen minutes, instead of one long one visualization exercise that can lend itself to distractions.

Imagination with reality.
We must ensure that the images we form in our minds are faithful to the reality we want to achieve. Bring forth the emotions and thoughts you experienced at that moment and focus on them.

Involve feelings and emotions.
There is something essential in visualizations. You must generate feelings consistent with what you are imagining. For example, if you create images of yourself being promoted at work, you should feel the emotion of the moment. Imagine giving a thank-you speech to your colleagues; that will certainly make the idea stick more deeply in your subconscious.

Look for the most positive images.
Once we manage to generate the images, we must review them and, if necessary, convert them. For example, notice if they lead you to a state of negativity or discomfort. In other words, we must work on our images until we get those that give us a signal indicating that they are the correct ones for that purpose.

RECOMMENDATIONS FOR EACH VISUALIZATION TO BE EFFECTIVE.

The first thing you must do is open your mind. If you do not have an open mind, this technique will not be effective. Only with 100% creative thinking will you be able to identify the opportunities that arise to meet your goals.

Always keep a positive mental attitude. Both the thoughts and the words will help you reinforce mental images, which eliminates the doubts and negativities that may arise.

Constancy is vital. Never give up. You have to believe in yourself and what you are capable of. Otherwise, you will never reach your established goals.

HOW DOES CREATIVE VISUALIZATION HELP US ACHIEVE SUCCESS?

Focuses our vision.
Our mind analyzes thousands of images and sounds every day. It only saves what is important to us from all this immense information and does it according to our tastes and desires. Some of that information is kept in memory, while the rest is reserved for further analysis. Your mind knows what is critical to you and only focuses on those parts of the whole.

This process is called the reticular filter or Reticular Activation System, and it is responsible for keeping our attention on our most immediate interests. For example, if you decide to buy a vehicle of a brand and a particular color, suddenly, you will begin to see cars of that color and model everywhere—something you didn't notice before.

This happens because we are predisposed to detect what you focus your attention on. So, what settles in your thoughts is detected in the physical world. You may have noticed that people who think only of difficulties live in them. The opposite is, always thinking positive and good things will start to happen to you.

So, you can decide which thoughts to lodge in your mind and which to remove. If you visualize what is necessary to reach your goals, your brain will become more alert to the opportunities related to them. If you visualize yourself speaking another language and engage the excitement of knowing another language, you will begin to see related opportunities. These will come to you because your brain will capture them and focus on the ones that are a priority, according to what you have seen in your visualizations.

It helps us root out bad content.
If you focus and reflect, you can conjure repeated patterns in your memory. For example, your partners always betray you, you end up in jobs that you hate, and so on. That is not just bad luck. It directly has to do with your thoughts. Remember, what is in our mind and the thoughts we implant in it will manifest in our life. Creative visualization will give you the tools to erase these thoughts and replace them with positive visions of what is good for you.

Match what you imagine to your reality.
Several studies and psychological analyses have shown that thinking about an action provokes a similar effect in the human body of carrying out said action. For example, if a person thinks that he or she is under the sea and cannot breathe, this person will begin to cough and gasp for air. So, if we imagine ourselves speaking in public with grace, ease, and eloquence, our brain will register that as truth. With practice, this would become an innate quality, especially if you used to be terrified of speaking in public.

HOW TO VISUALIZE CORRECTLY.

1. It is best to do it in a quiet space where no one will disturb you.

2. Get into a comfortable position.

3. Close your eyes and breathe calmly. Focus on your diaphragm as it inhales and exhales.

4. To train your mind, imagine a room you are familiar with. It could be your office. Focus on the distribution of the furniture, the color, the texture, and how the light enters through the windows. That will prepare you for when you make sustained visualizations.

5. Now, hold that scene. Visualize changes in it. For instance, change the arrangement of the furniture, the color of the walls, and place pictures on them. The idea is that you learn to modify the visualization as you see fit. It has to be as vivid as possible. Imagine yourself touching the objects or smelling them.

6. Now, it's time to introduce emotions into the scene. What do you feel at that moment? Happiness or discomfort? Prolong your feelings for a few minutes or seconds. With experience, you will learn to engage in longer visualizations, and with persistent practice, you will begin to see the changes.

Finally, you must understand that creative visualization is only part of the path that will take you to your goal. I want to clarify that, in addition to imagining and recreating a goal, you must make an effort to slowly take steps toward that goal so that it becomes a reality. Imagining a change in your life is not enough. You have to take action, and for that, I give you the tools that I have tried, and the tools that have made me the successful man I am today.

Better Dreams

My-mindguide.com

Chapter 12

Yoga: a miraculous method to achieve a truly restful night.

Yoga is a discipline that draws on ancient Hindu techniques combining physical exercise and breathing. It seeks communion between the mind and the body.

The origins of Yoga can be traced 3,000 years back. However, it was not introduced to Western culture until the early 20th century, although a few antecedents indicate its appearance by the late 19th century. In the United States, it became popular in the 1960s.

Much has been written about yoga, and many of you have likely caught a glimpse of this practice.

The benefits this discipline can bring to your life are multiple, and there are no adverse effects. Personally, being introduced to yoga was a turning point.

If your life is set at a hectic pace that leaves you stressed and tossing and turning at night, consider yoga. Although there are a few limitations, it is never too late to start.

For people who have difficulty falling asleep, yoga is a natural, non-pharmacological alternative that seeks to increase levels of mental and physical relaxation. Also, there is scientific evidence to back up these claims and to corroborate the positive effects of yoga.

HOW YOGA WORKS

Yoga is based on breathing exercises, while also stimulating flexibility through postures that seek to increase strength.

Yoga is often part of a strategy designed to increase one's level of relaxation. This strategy includes meditation exercises and mindfulness techniques.

It seems incredible that just a few decades ago, it was inconceivable that yoga was part of a therapy to improve the lives of people who complained of living in a constant state of stress, fatigue, and insomnia. However, studies have found that yoga was quite helpful in cases where people had symptoms of stress, sleep disorders, and depression. These exercises also proved to be significantly positive for cancer survivors.

The tension we experience during a busy day remains in our bodies unless we find a way to release it. Going to bed and sleeping for a few hours does not solve the problem, and after a while, we feel as though our rest is filled with knots of tension accumulating in our muscles.

Through a simple yoga session, we can virtually undo those knots and free ourselves from stress with feelings of immediate improvement. There is ongoing research looking to understand how yoga correlates to our sleep. The research in this area is focused on determining how this process that takes the body from tension to pleasant relaxation works.

Whether it's caused by a modification of the functions at the molecular level is not the most important aspect of this research. What *is* important is that the results are positive in all cases.

ARE THERE CHALLENGES FOR INDIVIDUALS PRACTICING YOGA?

A few people are temporarily or permanently unable to practice yoga:

- Pregnant women.
- People with injuries associated with sciatica.
- People with hernias and ulcers.
- Hypertensive people: These people can engage in light yoga, avoiding certain postures that affect cardiac processes.
- People with shoulder and spinal injuries.
- People who are recovering from surgery, at least until the physician gives explicit permission.
- People experiencing pain or injury to the ankles, hips, or wrists.

BENEFITS OF INCORPORATING YOGA IN OUR LIVES.

We usually approach yoga out of curiosity or because we are desperate. In both cases, more than 90% of the people who encounter this life discipline come back for more. The reason for this is, we can only improve our well-being by practicing this healthy discipline regularly.

Yoga:

✓ Improves relaxation in our body at the end of the day, making it easier to enter a state close to sleep. We also fall asleep easily, and sleep interruptions decrease.

✓ It strengthens the respiratory muscles, which is why people who snore can see a significant improvement with fewer episodes during bedtime.

✓ Yoga results in better cognitive processes.

✓ Yoga increases both flexibility and physical strength.

✓ Physical activity improves your ability to focus.

✓ Your energy increases as yoga becomes a part of your life.

✓ You will learn to become aware of your breathing process and improve it daily.

✓ By correcting posture, breathing, and relaxing the body, anxiety decreases.

Of course, there are benefits to practicing yoga on a spiritual level. This discipline allows us to look at our inner being through a process of self-knowledge that leads us to improve our character.

POSTURES THAT BENEFIT MIND-BODY RELAXATION.

These are easy-to-perform postures for beginners.

Balasana, or Child's Pose:

The pose resembles a child inside a mother's womb. This is where the individual sits on their knees, extends both hands so that they are parallel with the shoulders' width, leans fully onto the mat, placing both palms down and exaggerating the stretch so that it is felt throughout the body.

Run time: One to three minutes.

The Cow-Cat Pose (Chakravakasana):
Begin this position on the mat on your hands and knees. Separate your hands so that the distance is proportional to the width of your shoulders. As you inhale, begin lifting your head and allowing your pelvis to move upward, which will cause your lower back to round (cow). Exhale and move your body the opposite way, sinking your head and curving your back up (cat).

Run time: As many as you can do for one minute.

Savasana, or Corpse Posture:
The person lies face up on the mat. Once like this, the person remains motionless. This pose helps lead the body into a relaxed state.

Run time: five to ten minutes.

Vrikshasana, or Tree Posture:
In addition to relaxation, this posture seeks to restore balance.

The person stands with one leg bent, planting the sole of the foot on the weight-bearing leg while the hands are clasped at chest level, as if praying. The body is perfectly aligned.

Run time: The pose should be held for as long as you can before lowering your leg, breathing in, and repeating with the other leg.

Tadasana, or the Mountain Pose:
The person must stand with their weight perfectly balanced, distributed between both hips, the head in line with the pelvic area, and the chin parallel to the floor.

The arms can be at the sides or in a prayer position. It can be combined with visualization, evoking the roots of a tree emerging from both feet and settling firmly into the ground. While the position is kept, the breath must be steady, maintaining a rhythm that allows relaxation to be activated.

Run time: A minimum of five minutes.
These are some recommended exercises for relaxation. Keep in mind that it is wise not to push yourself too hard while your body adjusts to these exercises. You must get help from a suitable guide/teacher, expressing any conditions you may have, before starting therapy.

As a yoga teacher, I recommend yoga exercises for people seeking relief from symptoms and sleep disorders that have not been resolved by medication. I believe that—except for the limitations stated above—it is a therapy representing multiple benefits for those who practice it. Its effectiveness in cases of depression, stress, anxiety, and insomnia has been proven in several studies. And its positive effects continue to be discovered in patients with diseases, such as cancer and neuropsychiatric disorders. Thus, it can only improve our body and mind, bringing back our lost nights of rest.

Better Dreams
Doubt kills more Dreams
than failure ever has
My-mindguide.com

Chapter 13

One poor management of work stress can ruin your sleep.

In a world where everyone lives fast from day to day, daily activities do not escape this system in which work pressure and demands can be so many and so strong that they end up running our resources dry. That is how work stress appears.

We all have adaptive mechanisms, and can withstand certain types of pressure. However, we all also have a breaking point. In this chapter, I dive deeper into the requirements we are compelled to achieve in our workplace. When this situation is ongoing, an exhaustion effect is produced, and our cumulative capacity runs out. That is how we become blocked, and our minds stop implementing strategies to deal with stress. As a final consequence, our psychological states wither away.

These situations are more common than they may seem. Therapists state that more than 60% of patients who arrive stressed say they experience anxiety as a result of the intensity of the tasks required at work. As therapy progresses and the patient improves, it is necessary to work with various strategies to manage said anxiety and stress.

Stress management deserves analysis because it is often the first symptom of major illnesses, such as depression. That is why, if you are not consistent in working with a therapist or counselor, the symptoms of work stress will reappear, worsening the patient's overall clinical situation.

Symptoms, such as concentration and memory problems, appear as cognitive neuropsychological degeneration. This affects fundamental functions, such as attention, reasoning, memory, decision-making, and sleep problems.

Now, why do stress and not sleeping well affect mental functions? The answer lies in the constant supervision of our minds as a result of overload. Thus, we need to control all the chaos happening to us.

Moreover, our minds review all the scenes of the day just before we fall asleep. In fact, 90% of people think of negative or unhappy things before they sleep. This is something that the mind chooses to engage in, and it has a lot to do with the internal dialogue and how the person generally handles work stress.

Sadly, most people get carried away by the monster of anxiety. Not knowing how to deal with it, people allow it to prevent them from getting a good night's rest. However, some of that anxiety is the fault of evolution. Scientists have proven that the human brain suffers a so-called "anxiety peak," just when we are about to rest.

Gone are the times when we were hunter-gatherers, and although we no longer live surrounded by wild dangers and risks, the mind continues to react in the same manner, constantly processing threats. According to this archaic mind, the night is the ideal time to assess and detect situations or actions that could put us at risk and in danger.

So, when you go to bed and start going over your worries just before you sleep, the mind begins noticing red flags in the most insignificant aspects of life. Unfortunately, because of our mental evolution, the mind focuses more on problems rather than positive experiences. It does so naturally, to assess risks and plan strategies to adapt and survive in any environment.

HOW YOUR JOB STRESS AFFECTS YOUR SLEEP

For someone who goes to sleep physically and mentally exhausted, reviewing worries while in bed becomes all too easy. Jumping from rambling to examining the events that occurred in your office or any field of work is a one-way ticket to that dreaded insomnia. All this happens without being able to stop your mind and give it the much-needed rest to start a new day.

For these people, the stress caused by their work follows them home and gets into their bedrooms. The mind continues with its disastrous dialogue, taking inventory of possible assumptions and throwing around existential ideas, bringing forth sad or embarrassing memories.

If you identify with these scenarios, I want you to know that it is more common than you think. It affects millions of people around the world. But don't worry, there are strategies to handle it, and solutions that I will gladly share to help you overcome this type of downward spiral.

HOW TO PREVENT WORK STRESS FROM DAMAGING YOUR REST.

As we have already discussed, our mind makes it easier for us to remember negative events at night to find a solution and, thus, survive. To change this habit, it is necessary to hack your mind, which can be achieved through several strategies.

Meditation. If you want to change a negative habit, meditation is the basis of all treatment. It is meant to relax your body and mind so that you enter a state of lethargy before rest. Surely, relaxation through meditation slows us down from a busy day. It's like driving a car at high speed. If it stops abruptly, it will be catastrophic. We must brake gradually, decreasing our speed to a minimum to be able to stop peacefully.

This is achieved through meditation, so the body will be ready for rest, without rushing your mind. You can refer to Chapter 9 for various meditation techniques, where I explain the basics to achieve its benefits.

One of the techniques I recommend for sleeping is the following:

Take deep breaths, fill your lungs, and count to five. Then, exhale slowly. Repeat this three times.

Imagine yourself sitting on a quiet beach and trying to listen to the noise of the sea. Focus on the sound that the waves make when they crash against the stones and churn the water over and over again. As you lie down on the warm sand, see the clear sky and count down from ten to one.

Repeat this as many times as you need while softly and slowly moving your legs and arms to feel how the fine sand caresses you while you listen to the noise of the sea before you.

Generally, people fall asleep at some point in this visualization meditation. Counting down makes you focus on the numbers and lets your mind rest from negative thoughts as it prepares to rest.

Positive Visualizations. In Chapter 11, I emphasize how wonderful visualizations are for changing incorrect thinking patterns, false beliefs, and even harmful habits. You can also establish the visualization of well-deserved rest. Think that you are about to fall asleep without any issues. You just need to close your eyes.

The following visualization is like turning off the noise—in this case, the noise of your mind, but in a fictitious situation. It is useful for those days when you are exhausted, and anxious thoughts keep flowing through your mind.

Imagine there is a huge window in your room with a sliding panel, and on the other side of it, people are making a lot of noise—perhaps arguing loudly.

Visualize yourself getting up from your bed, going to the edge of the window, and touching its thick, cold panes. You listen to the chatter from the street and feel a gust of wind coming in and caressing your face. You also feel the smell of exhaust smoke from the vehicles circulating on that street. You take a deep breath and slam the window panel shut. It closes completely, and you stop hearing the noise. Only silence reigns in your room.

Now, imagine yourself returning to bed, placing your head comfortably on the pillow, and closing your eyes to sleep... No noise.

Soft Exercise: Yoga. In Chapter 12, I discuss the benefits of this ancient discipline. I experience the benefits of exercising through yoga every day and have qualified as a certified teacher by learning from the best and understanding why it has positive and therapeutic effects on people.

One of the qualities is that yoga incorporates mental and physical exercises, helping the practitioner achieve balance. People experience it first in their mind, then in their body. This new vision expands to the world around them, filling them with an intense inner peace.

Additionally, yoga provides increased and adequate conduction of the energy of the human body, which is why it provides great relaxation and a greater capacity for concentration.

Regularly practicing yoga exercises calms the nervous system, bringing the body into a more perceptive and healthy state of relaxation.

Since yoga relaxes the nervous system, it makes it possible to fall asleep better, which is ideal for days of high stress at work. Yoga demands concentration, so the mind soon forgets the harassing voices and focuses only on the movements and breaths. This causes our body to be more rested, so it recovers more energy. In addition, rest is excellent for the mind, making it much more lucid and attentive.

Moderate Sports Activity. Sports are beneficial for improving physical fitness and avoiding a sedentary lifestyle, and they are a wonderful method of relaxation and stress relief. However, if you cannot practice a sport, specialists recommend choosing moderate exercises instead. Stay away from exercises that demand a lot of cardio effort.

The most recommended low-impact exercises are walks, yoga, Pilates, and swimming. The movements associated with low-impact exercises are slower and smoother than those associated with high-impact exercises, such as running or lifting weights.

The important thing is to keep in mind that you should allow at least two hours to pass from the time you finish exercising until the moment you go to bed because the endorphins generated when doing any kind of exercise make our body alert, and we end with a high heart rate. I recommend letting the body rest for a while before taking a warm shower and drinking a cup of green tea, which makes it easier for us to prepare the body and mind for sleep.

Good nutrition. When we talk about foods that make us alert, coffee immediately comes to mind, but this is not the only drink that activates us, especially if we drink it at dinner time.

Soda interferes with falling asleep, as well. Chocolate is a stimulant that can either make you unable to fall asleep, or cause you to wake up early. Many people consume alcohol before bed because they think it helps them sleep better. However, that is entirely false because doing so would cause you to wake up after two or three hours, and it will be even more difficult to fall back asleep.

In general, carbohydrates make us sleepy, while proteins wake us up. For this reason, in addition to being more easily digestible, it is preferable to have a salad for dinner rather than any kind of meat.

DOES CHANGING JOBS HELP?

Work stress can be managed, but for many people, it is becoming increasingly difficult to do so. Many are trapped in situations that do not favor them, toxic work environments, poor working conditions, harassment, and so on.

Some people do not stop feeling anguish and hopelessness, despite attending therapy. If that is the case, it is time to start thinking about a more radical change in your life.

If work becomes a center of gravity in which thoughts cannot escape, then it is inevitably affecting the worker's emotional and physical health. An employee who suffers from psychological distress not only has poor performance during working hours, but also has an increase in absences due to illnesses associated with work stress. Job assignments pile up—or worse, you are constantly reprimanded by your superiors, creating a toxic and distressing cycle that is increasingly dangerous to your health.

The first thing you should keep in mind in these cases is that changing jobs is not considered a failure. On the contrary, you must take consider it the only possible option when your work threatens your physical and mental health.

Don't be afraid to keep looking for a better option.
Job searching can be an endeavor that lasts for years. However, if you can't stop working, you can't stop trying for something better, either. The only way to find an opportunity that suits you is to keep looking for it.

Most people take home the frustration, anxiety, and anger that a job they hate generates. However, this only causes that toxic environment to spread to all areas of your life when, in reality, it is only limited to a part of it.

Try to use all the resources I have shared with you to improve your life. Engage in activities you find pleasant. That will make it more difficult for certain ideas to transform into obsessive thoughts. This quality time you dedicate to leisure with your family, with your friends, or alone, will not only help you change the focus of your attention to more enjoyable things, but it will also give you the needed mental clarity to make decisions and solve problems you face.

Stay busy at work
When the activities we do are unpleasant, but also inescapable, we count the minutes until the day is over. However, this can only stretch out that feeling of boredom and misery throughout the day, making time move slowly.

Therefore, engage in your activities positively so the end of the day comes faster. Keep your productivity at an acceptable level to avoid more tension with your bosses and co-workers, especially if you work on a team.

Resolving the situation internally may be possible.
Sometimes, we can change things in our workplace, but we don't because we think it's not in our power to do so. Before you suffer more anxiety and frustration, find out about the company's policies. Use resources at your disposal to change what you do not agree with. You can talk to your bosses and make the changes in a way that favors both you and the entire staff. You can report illegal situations and much more.

Remember that what is at stake is your health, mental, psychological, and physical well-being. Sometimes, the pay of a toxic job is not enough to face the consequences that you will have to deal with in terms of health and emotional well-being.

Better Dreams

My-mindguide.com

Chapter 14

Rest habits and what you listen to influence your quality of sleep.

The time to rest and sleep is a renewing task for our entire body, meaning each part of your body must relax. Yet, every morning, millions of people wake up with neck, head, or lower back ailments and are more tired than they were when they went to bed the night before.

The best physiotherapists and physiatrists have studied this phenomenon, concluding that sleeping positions can be the cause for waking up stiffed instead of relaxed and bad-tempered the next morning.

These same specialists assure that some of these problems associated with poor sleep can be solved just by checking the position you're in when you sleep. Evaluating how you feel allows you to understand the advantages and disadvantages of sleeping in specific positions.

THE BEST POSITION TO SLEEP

In addition to being comfortable, the important thing is that your sleeping position does not excessively compress your joints or leave your muscles in an abnormally short or stretched position.

Three basic positions are described as most frequent when going to bed:

Face up. This is the most suitable way to go to bed. It balances the weight of the body, helps keep internal organs aligned, and prevents pain in your neck and back. It is recommended to use thin pillows and place a pillow under your knees when sleeping in this position to maintain the correct alignment of your back, thus avoiding lower back pain the following morning.

One of the drawbacks of sleeping on your back is that it may lead to acid reflux because the head is not higher than the stomach, generating a bubbling of gastric contents towards the esophagus. It is best to raise the head a few inches with a pillow of medium thickness to create a small angle while sleeping.

Fetal position. This position is most widely used and recommended, especially if you sleep on your left side. This position relieves ailments such as gastric reflux, snoring (obstructive sleep apnea), and shortness of breath. It also promotes lymphatic drainage, which is responsible for cleaning waste from the central nervous system.

It is a highly recommended position for people who suffer from lower back pain since it is neutral for the spine, preventing the weight from falling on it, while also reducing breathing difficulties. That being said, sleeping on your side creates pressure on your limbs, which can lead to muscle stress. However, the risk of this, along with the risk of compromised circulation, can be reduced by placing a pillow between your knees.

Multiple sleep studies agree that sleeping on the left side is the healthiest position for proper body alignment and rest.

Facedown. This is the least recommended sleeping position, especially for babies, since this position forces the spine into a position that is not in its nature, affecting the neck and cervical spine.

Sleeping on your stomach forces your body to maintain an unnatural posture for a long time. In this way, enormous pressure is applied on the entire body, particularly in the cervical area, and it involves muscles, tendons, nerves, and bones. This stress working all over the spine can cause problems such as tendinitis, low back pain, or neck pain.

Sleep research has revealed that we can change our sleeping position up to 36 times a night. Of course, this is influenced by our levels of stress, fatigue, noise, light, and all other possible stimulants that affect us during sleep, such as the temperature of the room, as well as the quality of the mattress and pillows.

Besides the fact that sleeping on your stomach is the least recommended position, doing it with your arms extended to your sides worsens the effect, thus increasing the compression on the nerves in your upper limbs.

When sleeping with several pillows, we intervene with the correct alignment of the neck and cervical spine, which produces cervical and lumbar pain. So, it is recommended to change the pillow if it is too high or rigid.

YOUR STATE OF HEALTH IS DECISIVE AT BEDTIME.

Healthy people have more freedom when sleeping because they can choose any position and experience minimal, standard, or baseline affects. However, that is not the case for patients with certain ailments. For them, it is necessary to choose one position that best favors their health.

Pregnant women generally choose to sleep on their side in the left lateral decubitus position. In this way, the vena cava is not compressed, which significantly improves circulation to the placenta.

Patients suffering from gastroesophageal reflux should avoid sleeping on their back and, if necessary, elevate the bed position to head level. The best alternative for them is to sleep in the left lateral decubitus position, like pregnant women.

People with lung difficulties or heart disease should sleep with two pillows to maintain a vertical tilt of the lungs and make breathing easier.

Low back pain is a fairly common condition, and its origin can be a strained muscle or ligament. People who have this condition should sleep on their back with minimal pillow elevation. Also, they can try sleeping on their side with their knees bent and separated by a pillow.

And finally, people who suffer from sleep apnea (snoring) should avoid lying in the supine position or on their back because that way, the tongue tends to move towards the pharynx, reducing the size of the pharyngeal opening and, therefore, minimizing the passage of air into the lungs.

It's important to be aware of which sleeping position is best for you and your unique needs. Remember that your hours of sleep are also the hours of regeneration of your whole organism. If you do this correctly, you will achieve optimal rest, therefore recovering energy more quickly.

RIGHT OR LEFT, WHICH IS THE BETTER SIDE?

The Journal of Clinical Gastroenterology published an article explaining that Dr. John Doulliard concluded that when we sleep on the left side of the body, we favor the lymphatic drainage of our body. The lymph drags the components that must be filtered by the lymph nodes, and it is on the left side in which the body finally expels them.

Resting on the left side of the body benefits the proper functioning of our digestive system. That facilitates a better production of gastric juices, and the secretion of pancreatic enzymes occurs without much effort. In this way, our digestive system is calmer, and its development occurs at a favorable time.

The heart also benefits from sleeping on the left side, because this vital organ of the human body is located on that side. Major veins, such as the aorta, leading from the heart to the abdomen, take an arching curve to the left, making it beneficial for proper circulation.

Another important organ, the spleen, is located to the left. It is a vital organ for the digestive, lymphatic, and immune systems. By sleeping on the left side, you are helping the body send natural fluids to the spleen so that it can do its job properly.

It is also paramount to be aware of the position the body takes during naps. Although they are short periods of sleep, naps are generally taken after a meal, and the position of the body influences good or bad digestion.

If you're worried about how you sleep, pay attention to how you wake up, even after a nap. You do not need to sleep all night in one position—we always move during the night. Simply return to the position that benefits you the most. It's just about changing the habit. Believe me, the conviction that a certain sleeping position will positively promote your health is the best incentive to adopt a healthy habit.

SLEEPING WITH BACKGROUND SOUNDS: WHY DO WE DO IT, AND HOW DOES IT AFFECT US?

An increasingly widespread habit among young people and adults is to fall asleep listening to music, a program, or a podcast. That, alongside the environmental conditions when sleeping, such as level of silence, darkness, temperature, and so on, have an important influence on our quality of sleep. These elements guarantee that we can sleep soundly and at the right time. However, many people adapt to sleeping with background noise.

The interesting thing is that far from being a fad, it has become a necessity for most of those who practice it, making it very difficult to fall asleep if they do not listen to something in the background.

WHY DO WE NEED TO SLEEP WITH NOISE?

Technology has been gaining ground, entering the bedroom, and accompanying us to bed. Now, it even follows us after we sleep. That is how an apparently harmless decision to listen to sounds all night became a hard-to-eliminate habit, creating a dependence not only on noise, but also on screens at bedtime.

This habit of sleeping with the mobile glued to us is difficult to abandon. Human beings are creatures of habit, and if we repeat the same patterns day after day, they become fixed in our minds and difficult to eradicate.

SOME ADVANTAGES OF SLEEPING WITH BACKGROUND NOISE

Sleeping with background noise can help mask other ambient noises, such as traffic, construction, nature, or the snoring of our bed partners, thus diluting the sounds we don't want to hear, and allowing us to focus on the sounds we *do* want to hear, like the television or our mobile devices.

This may help those who live in noisy places or who have night schedules that make it difficult to fall asleep with interruptions around them.

Moreover, some people find silence uncomfortable and disturbing. They fill that lack of noise that prevents them from falling asleep.

From a psychological point of view, individuals who hate silence are experiencing feelings of loneliness and fear and need all the virtual companionship they can get, which in today's society, can come from mobile devices or television.

DISCONNECTS THE MIND

Many people resort to background noise because it helps them disconnect their mind. The mental distraction that technology gives them helps them avoid negative thoughts, worries, and emotions that would otherwise keep them up all night, especially since one of the causes of insomnia is concentrating on things that worry or disturb us. So, being able to remove negative thoughts and experience silent minds while listening to music or our favorite program becomes very attractive.

WHITE NOISE, WHAT IS IT?

Neuroscientist, Jordi A. Jauset defines white noise[5] as "a sound signal that contains all the audible frequencies that exist, and all of them with the same amplitude."

White noise is persistent and repetitive, and integrates the entire spectrum of existing sound frequencies without highlighting them above others. The noise of the television (unintelligible dialogue) or untuned radio, the noise of the air conditioner (repetitive), a fan, rain without thunder, and ocean waves are examples of white noise.

It is becoming easier to find white noise recordings in our modern world. Even mobile apps generate up to ten hours of this sound. The purpose is to improve the sleep of people who find it difficult to sleep in the first place.

People who use it claim that it significantly improves their ability to relax when meditating and optimizes their concentration and cognitive skills. In addition, both adults and

---

5   https://www.sciencedirect.com/science/article/abs/pii/S1389945721002021

children use it. There are even sounds for babies that include heartbeats, thus emulating what infants heard in the womb.

Modern parents are increasingly turning to white noise to soothe their babies and increase quality and hours of sleep.

ADVANTAGES OF SLEEPING WITH WHITE NOISE.

The main advantage of sleeping with white noise is to help cover up other irritating sounds, such as traffic horns or music from noisy neighbors that seem disturbing to our rest.

Light sleepers and babies benefit from white noise, as other sounds are blocked or perceived with less intensity, preventing them from reaching the cerebral cortex.

Similarly, people who suffer from tinnitus can take advantage of this resource to achieve better quality sleep. The presence of continuous ringing in their ears tends to increase when going to sleep due to the prevailing silence, so, having a sound that blocks them, at least in part, can be a great relief for them.

DISADVANTAGES AND CONTRAINDICATIONS OF WHITE NOISE.

White noise is not an ideal and favorable solution for all people. It is especially harmful to those who suffer from sleep apnea, respiratory problems, but still, they use it.

Listening to white noise every night can damage our hair cells—the ones in charge of capturing sounds. In addition, the presence of such an unending noise will keep them active and prevent them from effectively carrying out the necessary regenerative work that takes place during sleep.

We must proceed with greater caution when implementing white noise in our babies' sleep routines. Exposing them to a very high volume could cause future damage to their hearing, which can later cause issues with language development.

HOW SHOULD WE PROCEED?

The use of white noise is something relatively modern, and not all scientists agree on adapting its use. However, I think it is a personal choice and should be used sparingly. If white noise is calming and puts you to sleep more quickly, try not to overdo it. Listen to it on nights when sleep is out of your reach and, of course, at the lowest volume possible, like a whisper.

This also applies to its use for children. If this noise calms your child's crying and puts him to sleep, find out first why the child is restless and do not rush to mask any symptoms that may indicate something is wrong. Ideally, you don't want to make white noise a habit or a firm part of their routine.

Remember what we talked about in this book: the habits of good rest rely on eating at specific times, eating healthy, exercising, practicing meditation combined with yoga, hypnotherapy, and visualizations. All these techniques will help you feel better, and in a short time, you will be able to sleep and rest properly.

If you have more complex problems or a sleep disorder, please do not hesitate to go to a specialist, who will be able to guide you in the necessary practices to recover your well-deserved rest. White noise may provide a temporary solution, but it is not a healthy long-term remedy.

Chapter 15

Lack of focus and poor concentration decrease your ability to produce successful ideas.

Neuroscientists focus on the brain and its impact on behavior and cognitive functions, but they also investigate what happens to the nervous system when people have neurological, psychiatric, or neurodevelopmental disorders. They also study the consequences of not sleeping and how it affects the concentration and mental capacity of those suffering from any of the aforementioned diseases.

Countless studies and experiments to discover how we control our mind have been conducted.

That being said, let's take a look at how our mind works. Consider these simple questions: Do you control your mind? Or does your mind control you? If you control your mind, we are going to do a test to determine whether that's true. Try not to think about anything. Try to clear your mind and silence your thoughts. What happened? Were you able to do this?

It's likely that something crossed your mind, and you tried to get your mind to understand that you are in control. You thought of commands like, "Don't think about anything, don't think about anything" and then noticed random thoughts popping into your head. That is normal. Our brains evolved to work that way. Due to a structure that scientists call the default neural network, our minds are always on, even when we do not want to think about anything. Even when we sleep.

The good side of this is that you can train your mind so that the default neural network works in a way that favors your goals, rather than having a mind that is self-sabotaging. If your default neural mode causes you to be sad, anxious, or unproductive, then we are going to learn how to change that so that your brain's default neural network works in favor of your concentration and productivity.

Our brain is our most complex organ. Until the early 20th century, when the electroencephalogram was invented, we knew very little about the actual workings of the brain. It was at this point that a study inadvertently made conclusions in this regard:

In that study, scientists asked a group of people to carry out mental tasks while electrodes and special machines monitored their brain activity. This monitoring was to be compared to a baseline level of brain activity. Therefore, the scientists also asked people to rest between tasks.

At that moment, something strange occurred. Scientists expected that brain activity would decrease at rest, but this was not the case. In fact, in some brain regions, brain activity increased during the resting period. At first, this was treated as a simple curiosity.

Many years later, a scientist named David Ingvar compared the results of tests that measured blood flow in the brain when people were resting. This is how he accidentally discovered that certain areas of the brain are activated as a network when we are supposedly resting. That is, when we are active, engaging the brain in mental activity, some areas are activated. However, when we are not active and are supposed to be resting, other areas of the brain are activated.

While we rest, our brain works on ideas, images, and things experienced during the day. That is why if you don't sleep properly, this function is wasted. That is why you have a hard time remembering and learning new things. This step is essential, but when you let it be the default network that guides your thoughts, you will wander through your memory without focusing on the present.

These thoughts that occur when we are not actively participating in any activity are what we define as the "default neural network." It is our standard way of thinking.

When your brain is in neural mode by default, your mind wanders, and you can't focus on the task at hand. When you are resting without actively participating in any mental activity, your brain remains active, but in standard mode by default. In this mode, your brain creates mental images, travels to the past, and plans for the future. This can be illustrated in moments when you're not doing anything, and suddenly, the best answer you could have given in a recent exam comes to mind, and no matter how much you racked your brain at the time, the answer did not come to you.

Whenever you are not actively using your brain to solve a problem, your mind begins to wander, travel through ideas, and generate stories. It is often during these ramblings that your mind produces creative solutions to problems. It is exciting and surprising, especially when the key suddenly appears without consciously thinking about the situation.

This is a positive aspect. However, it is not always good when the mind wanders. Reflect, for example, on people with depression, obsessive-compulsive disorders, and other mental disorders. These people generally have stronger connections between brain regions activated by the default neural network. People with Alzheimer's and autism spectrum disorder also have some dysfunctions in the default neural network.

Even in healthy people, excessive mind wandering can cause problems. A clear example is when you have to concentrate on a task, and your mind is distracted, following thoughts, digging into the past, or making plans for the future. That night, you find it difficult to sleep. You wake up distracted, having a hard time remembering the most immediate things that you would normally have no problem recalling. What has happened is that your mind has not rested, and the default neural network has not organized information during your hours of rest.

Some attitudes increase the activity of the default neural network, which makes our minds wander even more. For this reason, I will now give you two efficient tips on what you should do and what you should not do:

GET ENOUGH REST

The first thing you should do is sleep. Throughout these pages, I have emphasized how important it is to sleep, and how creating a suitable environment for a restful night is crucial to your body's functioning. In previous chapters, you found the mechanisms, causes, and consequences of sleeping the necessary hours in the right way.

Sleep is when the brain is resting and the production of hormones is balanced. That is how the memory can function optimally. Also, as you have already read, sleep strengthens neural connections.

At the University of Haifa in Israel, scientific specialists have verified these findings through a variety of experiments: During the REM phase of sleep, the hippocampus, the storehouse of our memory, is restored, transforming short-term memory into long-term memory and confirming the theory that a nap of at least 30 minutes in the middle of the afternoon helps fix skills and memories.

MEDITATE

Meditation is the most effective method to control the default neural network. Controlling our thoughts is not an easy task, since we are more emotional than rational beings. Despite this, there is a beneficial technique to manipulate the default neural network: focused attention meditation.

In focused attention meditation, you must choose a single thing to focus on, like your breath, an object in your room, or any image. The goal of meditating in this manner is to focus your attention solely on the one thing you chose for as long as possible. When you realize that you have lost focus on that one thing, you simply must refocus on it. It sounds easy in theory, but it is very complicated in practice. Generally, the thoughts that cause you to be unfocused involve the past or the future, and rarely have anything to do with the present moment.

The correlation between a lack of focus and the default neural network was demonstrated in a 2012 study.[6] This study asked several highly experienced meditators to practice focused attention meditation. Everything was closely monitored with images of brain activity. Whenever the volunteers lost focus and got distracted, they pressed a red button. Thus, the scientists could compare the moment of distraction with the image showing which brain regions are active. They were always the default neural network regions.

Therefore, the more you train your focused attention, the less dominant your default neural network will be. Even with constant practice of this type of meditation, thoughts will continue to arise in your mind. However, these thoughts no longer occupy your attention for a long time, and you will return to focus faster.

That shows that you are training and strengthening the brain regions responsible for concentration. These regions form the so-called executive network since they are responsible for cognitive control. It is as if the organizational network were a positive brain activity to perform tasks, and the default neural network was an off-brain activity to perform tasks.

____
6   https://pubmed.ncbi.nlm.nih.gov/21782031/

The more you practice focused attention meditation or any type of meditation, the stronger the executive network will be, and the weaker the default neural network will become. In Chapter 9, you will find easy-to-start guidelines for the principles of meditation that I have taught my students for years, and have been proven to be effective.

The incredible benefits of meditation will teach your mind to wander less, making it less susceptible to distraction. The default neural network mindset will no longer be in charge, and instead, your brain will be empowered to focus whenever needed and on whatever needed, increasing your productivity and improving decision-making.

The brain is the most complex organ we have. Thanks to multiple studies and surveys, scientists have been able to reveal, more and more, how our mind works.

The default neural network distracts your mind when you are not consciously involved in mental activity, but focused meditation practice reduces distractions. There are other techniques rooted in and proven by neuroscience that can give you more control over your brain:

Negative perfectionism.
Perfectionists give a thousand thoughts to one issue, thinking of hundreds of angles to make it perfect and up to standard. Through that process, they spend too much time on a given project, and their thoughts do not stop wandering and exploring the possible causes and consequences of why the project may be rejected.

To break this cycle and stop overthinking, we must ask the following questions: Why can't I finish this project once and for all? What is my real fear? You will find the answers within you. In addition to helping you stop rambling and take action, these questions keep you away from thoughts that have nothing to do with the present moment.

Stop wanting to control everything.
Take a step back and explore a different perspective when you find yourself thinking about a thousand things at once. Instead, ask yourself: Am I thinking about something beyond my control? Or is it something that I can control?

It could be that you are stuck in traffic and you cannot do anything to get around the problem at the moment, so, guide your thoughts towards something that you *can* control, instead. You can use your time stuck in traffic to get through your to-do list, listen to an audiobook, check out classes for a language you want to learn, or just take deep breaths and let your mind rest for a bit before you get to your office or meeting place.

Let time be on your side.
If the situation is under your control, the next step is to identify and isolate the problem and give yourself a time limit to fix it. Focus on finding a way to solve it, or at least establish a strategy so it can be solved within the time you've allocated.

Getting your default neural network to control your mind is not an easy task, but every time you focus on the present, you take a firm step toward stopping your thoughts from wandering and being in charge of your mind. Think of solutions and actions that fall within the realm of your control.

Chapter 16

Improve your mood and your performance to be happier.

The Johns Hopkins University School of Medicine published a study on behavior. The study demonstrated that people who do not regularly sleep the recommended number of hours experience minimal positive emotions, are less happy, and have higher rates of negative emotions, such as anger.

Sleeping the necessary hours continuously and without interruptions is essential. Otherwise, your rest period does not go involve the different states required to achieve a refreshing sensation. This is why people who have this problem wake up in a lousy mood and spend the rest of the day miserable.

HOW DOES GOOD SLEEP AFFECT HAPPINESS?
Biologically, happiness demands naturally activated chemicals, such as endorphins, serotonin, dopamine, and oxytocin. In this way, our body generates different responses to situations, including calm, laughter, a desire for affection, and the feeling of enjoyment.

In addition, good sleep is essential for the body to function properly. At the stage of physical rest, the brain works intensely to consolidate the information encountered during the day, renewing itself for the following day.

We face many issues if we do not do everything possible to rest the necessary hours (7-8 hours in adults). As all studies posit, interrupted rest produces hormonal imbalances, increases stress levels, changes mood, reduces concentration, modifies appetite, and intensifies physical ailments. All these imbalances in the body's natural chemical system are involved in the sensation of happiness—to a greater or lesser degree.

If a person does not sleep enough or does not do it correctly, they will not appreciate the positive stimuli in their maximum splendor. A rested person can feel very happy when receiving stimulation, such as a hug, but they will not do so in the same way if they slept poorly, thus meaning they will not experience a high level of happiness.

WHAT FACTORS ARE TRIGGERED SO THAT THE INDIVIDUAL IS UNHAPPY?

Lack of control of emotions
Nowadays, sleep has almost become optional. There is a belief that you can—and, at times, even should—stop sleeping properly if you want to achieve success. But this is far from the truth. Not respecting our hours of rest generates problems of all kinds and increases any underlying problems that we may already suffer from.

When the required hours of sleep are not reached, or it is impossible to sleep soundly, a person is left feeling on edge.

That is how a person becomes highly irritable or especially sensitive to any type of stimulus. It is clear that not sleeping well considerably affects our state of mind.

A person with misplaced emotions can explode at the slightest touch. It is common for a person to react with anger in response to basic interactions or dialogue with others. There is one primary culprit for this: lack of sleep.

Irrational and primal behaviors
Many studies have shown that taking hours off sleep to perform any activity also comes with its consequences, all of which severely affect the prefrontal lobe, the area that regulates emotions. Lack of sleep leads to more irrational and primal responses.

Although it is popularly believed that lack of sleep leads to a state of weakness and passivity, the opposite is true. People who don't get enough sleep do not become increasingly passive, rather 60% of these people become more reactive, violent, and uncontrolled.

For someone experiencing this issue, it is much more challenging to change limiting beliefs and replace them with new, self-serving beliefs. The mind hacking that I discussed in Chapter 13 becomes almost impossible because the mind of someone who only sleeps four hours a day will inevitably be filled with erratic thoughts and false beliefs such as, "I must do things well to deserve the approval of others"; "Others must act considerately and fairly"; and "Life should provide me with favorable and easy conditions so that I can get what I want, effortlessly."

Difficulty making decisions
All thought patterns are significantly altered by lack of sleep. The consequence is that processing information in the short and long term becomes difficult, making decision-making almost impossible. A study revealed that physicians' mistakes rise to more than 400% in the health sector if they work more than a continuous 24-hour shift.

The work schedules of these professionals must be evaluated and reassessed because sometimes, they inadvertently do more harm than good. And this extends to all people who do work where concentration is essential. They can put their lives and the lives of others at risk.

POSITIVE CONSEQUENCES OF GETTING ENOUGH REST

- While we sleep, the brain processes information, learning from the day's experiences and forgetting negative memories, allowing us to rest more authentically and productively.

- We have more resources to combat stress and irritability when we are rested.

- When we sleep well, appetite hormones are balanced, maintaining an ideal weight, and positively affecting our self-esteem at an emotional and psychological level.

- Having the necessary hours of rest makes it more likely that our sexual appetite will increase.

When sleep and wakefulness occur in harmony, our body functions properly. Sleeping well improves our quality of life. There is nothing to lose in regulating sleep and much to gain.

Not everyone understands that lack of rest can affect their happiness. Not sleeping well causes us to perceive and process happy moments incorrectly. A person may be living the best moments of their life but will not be able to fully enjoy them if they do not prioritize their quality and quantity of sleep.

Resting well and getting enough sleep translates to a healthier life—one where we can smile broadly, knowing our welfare is not in a faraway future, but here, in the present.

Conclusion

Along time ago, I came to a crossroads where I had to choose between adopting a positive and enthusiastic attitude, in which I sought to see the bright side of things by focusing on opportunities, or adopting a negative or realistic attitude. In the end, I decided to focus on the positive. I overcame many obstacles, and today, I share with my readers all the topics I consider relevant to achieving success in life.

Of course, health is essential to me, especially as a hypnotherapist who has helped thousands of people succeed and achieve optimal health. I know that getting enough sleep is the panacea for a better life from every point of view.

I want to thank you for accompanying me on this journey. My purpose has been to make you aware of how inadequate sleep can affect the brain. Insomnia is more dangerous than believed, since it negatively affects our thoughts and memory, while also reducing our cognitive abilities.

In these pages, I hoped for the reader to become aware of how our physical health is affected by poor sleep, in terms of our risk for diabetes, obesity, and heart disease, all of which are a result of a weak immune system due to hours of insomnia or sleeping half of what specialists advise.

Not sleeping properly is often a product of the modern world that is violently fast-paced, and we assume that we have to be glued to the mobile or tablet for as long as possible to avoid missing "anything important." Such an attitude has created a new generation of technological outcasts—people who go through life with feelings on the surface, erratic emotions, and foul humor, preventing them from the most fundamental thing that human beings must have: happiness.

I sincerely hope you have found an incentive on these pages to start making a change in your life. I hope that you take some of the tools I introduced, such as visualizations, meditation, yoga, and positive thoughts, to help you get out of the darkness and failure in which those who do not sleep frequently find themselves. These people have even lost the ability to eradicate the false beliefs that keep them in a place where they cannot complete the simplest of goals.

Here, I show you that it is possible to hack your mind, change your paradigm, rewire your brain, and implement strategies that will take you to the next level of your life. A rested mind can overcome any obstacle, taking you wherever you want to go.

If you enjoyed this book and would like to read about other topics that have changed my life, please check out my new books on Amazon or my website: www.my-mindguide.com.

Also, let's stay connected on social media. Please drop a line on Facebook or Instagram, and stay tuned for updates! You're welcome to share your thoughts with me directly, as well: gassner@my-mindguide.com. In return, I'll send you a gorgeous infographic that you can cut out and frame.

Also, please leave a review on Amazon, as this will help me reach an even broader audience.

Thank you so much for your time, insight, and an undying hunger for knowledge!

Thank you to all my colleagues, clients, friends, and family members, who have all contributed to what and who I am now.

Thank you, Gabriel Palacios, a Swiss bestseller author, the king of hypnotherapy. He taught this old fox new tricks, letting me deep-dive into the mystery of hypnotherapy. I learned so much along the journey, and am now a certified master-hypnosis coach and conversation coach myself.

Thank you to the fantastic teachers of SAMYANA/Bali who trained me to become a certified yoga and meditation teacher.

And last but not least, thank you to my master-teacher, Eckhard Wunderle, who's close to a saint to me. He introduced me to the world of meditation and let me discover all the wonders it has to offer. I couldn't be prouder of having received my meditation teacher certification directly from him at the Institut für Spirituelle Psychologie.

Peace, love, and happiness to all of you—until next time!

Authors portrait

Kurt Friedrich Gassner has worn many hats throughout his lifetime, including but not limited to serial entrepreneur, Creative Director, Meditation Teacher, Licensed Hypnotherapist, and more recently, self-improvement author. Leveraging his treasure trove of experiences and in-depth knowledge of psychology, he provides his readers with the tools they need to unlock their infinite potential.

As a prolific self-help writer, Kurt has authored the following books: *The Art of Forgiveness*, *Lie or Die*, *Soul-Match*, *Can You Inherit a Poisoned Mind?* and *The Power of Poverty*. He also authored a best-selling children's book in German-speaking countries and has over 20 books underway.

When it comes to enduring success, Kurt understands that financial prosperity isn't the only aspect one should strive for. He may be a self-made millionaire, but what really transformed his life is mastering his unconscious mind. Perseverance, personal power, self-awareness, and learning from past mistakes have all been key ingredients to bringing his dreams to fruition—and he strives to impart that wisdom onto others through his writing.

During his spare time, Kurt Friedrich Gassner is either traveling across the globe, golfing, biking in the Alps, hiking, or spending quality time with his loved ones. For the last 37 years, he has been happily married and he is the father of two successful children. Presently, he resides in both Munich, Germany, and Kirchberg, Austria.

OTHER BOOKS BY THE AUTHOR

BÜCHER VOM AUTOR IN DEUTSCHER AUSGABE

OTHER BOOKS BY THE AUTHOR

My-mindguide.com
NEVER APPLIED
THE ULTIMATE POWER TO THINK AND ACT OUT OF THE BOX
KURT GASSNER

My-mindguide.com
NIEMALS BEWORBEN
DER ULTIMATIVE SCHLÜSSEL ZU UNKONVENTIONELLEM DENKEN
KURT GASSNER

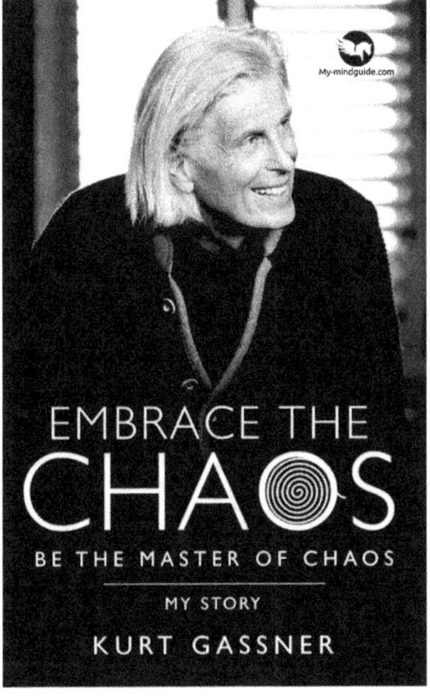

My-mindguide.com
EMBRACE THE CHAOS
BE THE MASTER OF CHAOS
MY STORY
KURT GASSNER

My-mindguide.com
DAS CHAOS BEHERRSCHEN
WERDE MEISTER DES CHAOS
MEINE GESCHICHTE
KURT GASSNER

My-mindguide.com
ECKO
FIRED FOR SUCCESS?
TRUE STORIES AND MANAGEMENT LESSONS
FOR OUR TOUGH CHANGING TIMES
KURT GASSNER

My-mindguide.com
ECKO
WEGEN ERFOLG GEFEUERT
Eine wahre Geschichte über das Scheitern in Unternehmen und
was junge Führungskräfte aus einer Fehlerkultur lernen können.
KURT GASSNER

My-mindguide.com
Unlocking
The Healing
Power of Pets
What Pets Can Tell You About Your Soul
KURT GASSNER

My-mindguide.com
Heilkraft
Unserer
Lieblinge
Was Haustiere über Ihre Seele verraten können
KURT GASSNER

My-mindguide.com
THE BLISS OF STRUGGLE
WINNING STRATEGIES FOR DEMANDING TIMES
KURT GASSNER

My-mindguide.com
STARK DURCH „STRUGGLES"
DAS IDEALE MINDSET, UM KRISEN ZU MEISTERN
KURT GASSNER

My-mindguide.com
LIE LYING & LIAR
A LIE HAS NO LEGS BUT IT HAS WINGS
KURT GASSNER

My-mindguide.com
LÜGE LÜGEN & LÜGNER
EINE LÜGE HAT KEINE BEINE, ABER SIE HAT FLÜGEL
KURT GASSNER

BORN
in the
COLD
Liebe und Aufmerksamkeit in der Wachstumsphase eines Kindes
KURT GASSNER

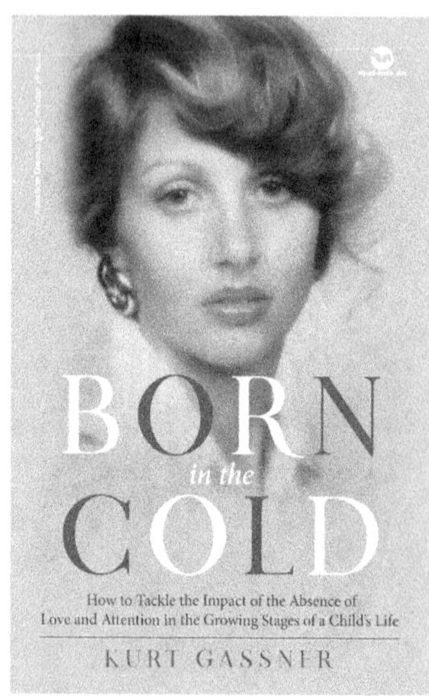
BORN
in the
COLD
How to Tackle the Impact of the Absence of
Love and Attention in the Growing Stages of a Child's Life
KURT GASSNER

SOPHIAS WUNDERWELT
Kirchberg & Kitzbühel in den Kitzbüheler
Alpen, Tirol, Österreich
10 ERZÄHLUNGEN
KURT GASSNER

SOPHIA'S WONDERWORLD
Kirchberg-Kitzbühel in the Austrian Alps
10 TALES
KURT GASSNER

BESTSELLING AUTHOR OF
The Art Of
FORGIVNESS
AMAZON
#1
BESTSELLER
My-mindguide.com
A practical guide for
self healing and
overcome past traumas
The Art Of
FORGIVNESS
KURT GASSNER
The Art Of
FORGIVNESS
KURT GASSNER